Dog Tales

Dog Tales

Hundreds of Heartwarming, Face-Licking, Tail-Wagging Tales about Dogs ...

... from Hundreds of People Who Love Them!

Hundreds of Heads Books, LLC

ATLANTA

Cover photograph by Unlisted Images, Inc.

Cover and book design by Elizabeth Johnsboen

Library of Congress Cataloging-in-Publication Data

Dog tales : hundreds of heartwarming, face-licking, tail-wagging tales about dogs.
   p. cm.
 ISBN-13: 978-1-933512-09-9
 1. Dogs--Anecdotes.
 SF426.2.D646 2007
 636.7--dc22

2007027030

HUNDREDS OF HEADS™ books are available at special discounts when purchased in bulk for premiums or institutional or educational use. Excerpts and custom editions can be created for specific uses. For more information, please email sales@hundredsofheads.com or write to:

HUNDREDS OF HEADS BOOKS, LLC
#230
2221 Peachtree Road, Suite D
Atlanta, Georgia 30309

ISBN-10: 1-933512-09-1
ISBN-13: 978-193351209-9
Printed in U.S.A.
10 9 8 7 6 5 4 3 2 1

CONTENTS

According to one popular theory, a young couple thinking about having a child should first get a dog. The responsibility of having a dog—feeding, discipline, and elimination training, along with so much else—will prepare the couple for the immense responsibility of childrearing.

But having a dog in the family is really quite different. For one thing, many dog owners would argue that newborn puppies are much cuter than newborn babies. For another, when the child grows, he or she increasingly separates from the parents, and in fact takes delight in arguing with them and insulting them. Instead, as a dog grows, as it is trained, and as the master is trained to the dog's life, the dog grows ever fonder of his "parents." Separating—let alone arguing or insulting—is rarely an option for either party. Of course, there are other differences, too: seldom do grown children attack the mailman, pee on furniture, or beg for food during dinner. Like our children, dogs are part of our family. We love them whatever they do.

That's what this book aims to celebrate. Through stories from hundreds of dog lovers across the country, we learn about dogs that have permanently altered the lives of their humans. In this book, you'll find real stories of dogs that make us laugh, save lives, sense danger, befriend other species, and overcome amazing obstacles. And because this situation eventually comes to all of us, you'll hear how other owners finally said goodbye to their best friends. The stories remind us of how much our canine companions mean to us. What would we do without them?

Hundreds of Heads Books

Meet Your Dog

Is there such a thing as love at first sight? Ask the contributors to this chapter and they'll tell you they know it exists. They take one look at those big, sad eyes; that stubby little tail vibrating with excitement; those long, silky ears; and they know resistance is futile.

There's a dog—sometimes two, or three—for everybody. And often, the dog chooses its human, not the other way around; read about Tobi the toe-licker and you'll see what we mean. But however it begins, the bond between dog and owner soon feels as if it was always meant to be.

WE FOUND MONTY AT A SHELTER in a small cage with a beagle. My husband took him out and placed him on the floor, and it was love at first sight. Not that "isn't-he-so-cute; Golden-Retriever-puppy" kind of love. It was more like the "he's scrawny, sad-looking, and has a really bad shave" kind of love. My first thought was that he was a little ugly. But I just couldn't keep my heart from melting. I like the Charlie Brown Christmas trees and the bumpiest, misshapen pumpkins, so it only makes sense that I would love that flea-ridden mutt.

—BETH BROWN
CINCINNATI, OHIO
🐕 MONTY, TERRIER-POODLE MIX, 5

● ● ● ● ● ● ● ● ●

DO NOT GO TO A SHELTER unless you are ready to get a dog because you will fall in love. When we got mine, we weren't looking for a dog but we saw a black lab with a tag that said "Not good with children. Not housebroken." But the dog just looked at us, head cocked to one side. We took him out to play and he was great with my 10-year-old niece. We think the previous owners just wrote that as an excuse to get rid of him. So when we heard, "This guy will be put down tomorrow," I was like "No, he's not." We brought him home.

—KARL
NORRISTOWN, PENNSYLVANIA
🐕 BLACK LABRADOR RETRIEVER, 3

WE WERE SMITTEN WITH OUR DOG, LULU, the second we saw her. We'd noticed a sign painted on a cardboard box saying that Labrador puppies were for sale, and we went to the house to pick one out. Lulu clambered over all of her sleeping siblings to jump into our hands, and we just had to take her home. However, we soon realized the error of our ways; she didn't sleep for about two years!

—MARISKA VAN AALST
EMMAUS, PENNSYLVANIA
🐕 LULU, LABRADOR, 7

• • • • • • • • •

I WAS LEAVING FOR WORK ONE MORNING during a thunderstorm. I saw this drenched dog in my front yard, shaking like a leaf. I started talking to him; I had no idea if he was vicious or not. My neighbor said the dog had been around the neighborhood so I figured he must live nearby and would eventually go home. He wouldn't stop following me as I was trying to leave, so I went in the house and got a biscuit. While he was busy chomping, I drove away. As I approached an intersection, I glanced in my rearview mirror: There was this dog tearing after my car! I had to put this wet, yucky animal in my car and drive back home. I just fell in love.

—KATHY GERMANA
FARMINGVILLE, NEW YORK
🐕 LUCKY, MIXED BREED, 7

PEPPER WAS A STUNNINGLY BEAUTIFUL, black Shar-Pei rescue. I took her home from a veterinarian's office. My boyfriend, Bob, and I were driving to meet her when we got a flat tire. Fortunately, we were just across the street from the animal hospital and Bob agreed to change the tire while I went to meet Pepper and the rescue lady. Pepper was not impressed with me; she sniffed me and let me hold her leash but she really didn't bond instantly with me. I decided to take her across the street to meet Bob and see how she reacted to him. He was still changing the tire when we got to him. Well, Pepper took one look at him and fell in love on the spot. She ran right up to him and gave him a big sloppy kiss on the face, with her tail wagging a mile a minute. I adopted the dog and married the man.

—LORA
SEAFORD, NEW YORK
🐕 CHOWDER, 5 🐕 GINGER, 2
🐕 BELLO, 6, CHINESE SHAR-PEIS

. . . .

I GOT SADIE WHEN I WAS WORKING downtown at a parking lot. A truck driver got out of his truck and came up to me and asked me if I knew anyone who wanted a puppy. Then Sadie got out of the truck and came up to me, and I knew I had to have her. She was six months old. I've had her for about six years.

—MATTHEW SKILES
CINCINNATI, OHIO
🐕 SADIE, CHOW CHOW, 6

THE YORKIE PUP WE GOT was the last one left in the litter, and she was just sitting there, shaking, doing everything the book said not to choose. But of course I was going to take her: I wanted a female and had been on the waiting list for a long time. And of course, she's turned out just fine.

—SIDNEY
MINNEAPOLIS, MINNESOTA
🐕 DAISY, YORKSHIRE TERRIER, 1

• • • • • • • •

FOZZY, three years old, lives in Roseville, Minnesota.

• • • • • • • •

MY WIFE FOUND A RHODESIAN RIDGEBACK in an animal shelter through the Internet. He had two broken legs and mange, and had to have multiple eye surgeries. I thought it might be a bad idea to adopt him, but we've had Mr. Robinson for about five years now and he's a good dog.

—PATRICK WALKER
HENDERSON, KENTUCKY
🐕 MR. ROBINSON, RHODESIAN RIDGEBACK, 11
🐕 SIBERIAN HUSKY, 12

MY DOG WAS THE RESULT of years of scheming. Despite my husband's insistence that we should not have a dog yet, as soon as we moved into a place that was big enough for a dog (and had a convenient doggie door and fenced-in backyard), I was dragging him to the SPCA to pick out the pooch of my dreams. We wandered around and looked at the cages. A medium-sized sheltie caught our eyes. Standing there—feet splayed, tongue panting, tail wagging—she looked like the happiest dog I'd ever seen. We reached our fingers through the cage to pet her, and she immediately turned and pressed her body against the cage to give us maximum petting exposure. Our hearts broke, and we knew she was ours.

—SHAROLYN WIEBE
VANCOUVER, CANADA
🐕 CASEY, SHELTIE, 9

· · · · · · · · ·

When we went to the breeder, Spike came up to each of us and licked us and wouldn't leave our sides. Apparently, we belonged to him.

—VERONIQUE N.B. SMITH
HUME, VIRGINIA
🐕 SPIKE, MINIATURE AUSTRALIAN SHEPHERD, 3

WHEN WE WERE LOOKING for a Golden Retriever, we met a breeder who had a top working Golden, but when the woman let him out of the crate, he turned circles for five minutes, and I thought, "I can't live with that!" You'll find breeders at the dog shows and they'll have dogs that win, but lots of times you can't live with them! It's very clear. But when you find a breeder whose dog wags its tail and licks your hand, ask where they got their dog and ask if there are any breeders in the area who have a similar line of dogs.

—PATRICIA
MINNEAPOLIS, MINNESOTA
🐕 GOLDEN RETRIEVER, 2
🐕 SHETLAND SHEEPDOG, 13

• • • • • • • •

MY MOTHER DECIDED TO GET this fancy dog: a Borzoi, or Russian Wolfhound. I thought she was crazy. I'm not the biggest dog person to begin with, but if you're going to get a dog, I figured, you should get it from the pound. So she paid $500 for this dog, and my brother and I gave her hell for it. But I'm in love with this dog. He's amazing: so sweet, with a personality that's from another world, like a unicorn or something. The dog is basically mine as much as hers now; I have him all the time. And while I still think the noble thing is to go to the pound, I understand that some breeds have exactly what someone wants, and that some people need to go for that.

—B.R.
ATLANTA, GEORGIA
🐕 BORZOI, 6

TOBI took the initiative and selected her owner during a temporary stay in a North Carolina animal shelter.

BARBARA LAVALETTE (OWNER)
RALEIGH, NORTH CAROLINA

HAVE YOU EVER SEEN THE MOVIE *Funny Farm* with Chevy
Chase? He buys a dog he names Yellow Dog that runs
away as soon as he brings him home. The same thing
happened to me. We bought this Collie from a friend and
as soon as we let him out of the car he bolted. He was
found on the other side of town two days later. We were
lucky because we didn't even have ID tags on him yet.
We figured we had time for that. Put the tags on the dog
as soon as you get it. You just can't be too safe.

—JANE TABACHKA
GREEN MOUNT, VIRGINIA
COLLIE

I found my dog shivering underneath a
pile of flotation cushions on the boat
docks. I lured her back to our campsite
with snacks, and ended up keeping her
for years. She was one of best pets
I've ever had.

—BONNIE SMITH
MANCHESTER, MISSOURI
ENGLISH SPRINGER SPANIEL, 13

THE NAME GAME

WE HAVE A FRENCH FRIEND who told us that "Medor" is the stereotypical French dog's name—sort of like Spot. So we named our dog Medor. Since we live in America, it seems unusual and exotic, and only the occasional French person we encounter gets the joke.

—A.L.
BOSTON, MASSACHUSETTS
🐕 MEDOR, MIXED BREED, 3

• • • • • • • •

I THOUGHT IT WAS SO CUTE AND INNOVATIVE when my parents got a Golden Lab and named her Maggie. Then one day, I was home visiting them, and I took Maggie to the park. Somebody next to me started calling "Maggie," and her own Golden Lab ran to her. I swear there were half a dozen Golden Labs named Maggie. Next time my parents should visit the park first.

—SUSAN
CHICAGO, ILLINOIS
🐕 MAGGIE, GOLDEN LABRADOR, 13

• • • • • • • •

IF YOU LET YOUR YOUNG CHILDREN CHOOSE your pet's name, be prepared for names like "Dipsy-Dipsy Doo-Doo." We call her Dippy for short.

—HEIDI
CHICAGO, ILLINOIS
🐕 DIPSY-DIPSY DOO-DOO, MIXED BREED, 7

WHEN I WAS FIRST MARRIED, my wife and I bought a total mutt. He was so many breeds mixed together that you couldn't begin to guess at his ancestry. So we called him Alboe: A Little Bit Of Everything.

—COLIN MCDOUGLE
CANFIELD, OHIO
🐕 ALBOE, MIXED BREED, 10

• • • • • • • •

THINK ABOUT WHAT IT WILL BE LIKE to scream your dog's name out loud. You might even want to practice first. I was all set to name my dog Bean, which I thought was cute, because she was shaped like a little Jelly Bean. But I live in an area with a lot of Latinos, and my friend pointed out that screaming that word might come across as something sort of derogatory. So I named her Jelly instead, and I can scream out, "Jelly, Jell-Jell!" to my heart's content.

—K.B.
SAN FRANCISCO, CALIFORNIA
🐕 MIXED BREED, 6

I SAW MY COWORKERS HUDDLED around a small dog bundled in a towel. They'd found him wandering around the parking lot. His bulging eyes were really gunky; one had a protruding gland and white specks. Let's just say he was not appealing. They took him to a nearby shelter, and I went to visit him. He was matted and filthy, staring straight ahead while another dog humped him. When I talked to him, he wasn't responsive to me. I went back the next day and took him for a short walk. He kept pulling me all over. But the day after that I decided to adopt him. I guess I felt sorry for him; I thought no one would want him because he was an older dog and such a mess. He cleaned up nicely; now he's constantly by my side.

—MARIE BALL
LINDENHURST, NEW YORK
🐕 BOCCI, 10 🐕 BELLA, 4

• • • • • • • • •

MY COWORKER WAS SUPPOSED TO GIVE ME my Lhasa Apso puppy six weeks after she was born, but she surprised me a week early. She took a long lunch break and came back 30 minutes before work was over with a little box. We went to the lunchroom, and I opened the box and saw this itty-bitty thing with big ol' pretty eyes. I took her out quickly and hugged her little body. I felt like I had actually given birth!

—EVETTE WILLIS
CHICAGO, ILLINOIS
🐕 JAZZY, LHASA APSO, 1

WHEN WE FOUND MY DOG, POPPY, at the Humane
Society, he looked like a sad-eyed rug lying there quietly
among the other dogs, who were making a racket. He'd
been so abused that he could only crawl around on his
belly. Completely unresponsive on the way home, Poppy
buried his nose in the backseat of the car. But when we
arrived, he shot out of the car and ran straight to our
door. Somehow, Poppy knew he was home.

—NIKKI GLENN
ST. LOUIS, MISSOURI
🐕 POPPY, MIXED BREED, 4

• • • • • • • •

MY WIFE ASKED ME TO JOIN HER FOR LUNCH on a Saturday
afternoon when she was working. I knew something was
up when she asked me to lunch; normally she would
rather eat rats than have lunch with me. As soon as the
elevator stopped on her floor and I heard the howling, I
knew we were getting a dog. Her company was hosting
an adopt-a-pet event, and when we entered the auditorium
she bullied some young children out of the way, exposing
the skinniest, crazy-eyed Husky I had ever seen. The
attendants told us what an obedient and wonderful dog
he was, and how great he was in the car. Needless to say,
he has never once been obedient in 10 years and is not
allowed in the car anymore. I never did get lunch.

—JOE ANDERSON
ST. PAUL, MINNESOTA
🐕 REGGIE, HUSKY, 11

BUSTER CAME TO ME AS A RESCUE. He was a year-and-a-half-old Rottweiler with ear problems. The people who bought him from the breeder realized they didn't want him when they saw that it took three technicians and one vet to hold him—basically manhandle him—just to clean his ears. He wasn't an aggressive dog; it was just painful for him. The breeder asked me to evaluate him before she tried to give him to someone else. I said, "He's not going anywhere, he's staying with me!"

—JANICE
SAN DIEGO, CALIFORNIA
🐕 TOKEN, 4 🐕 DOLLY, 1, COCKER SPANIELS
🐕 EMME, 5 🐕 BUSTER 🐕 VITA, ROTTWEILERS

• • • • • • • •

MY HUSBAND AND I WENT TO THE POUND one day to pick out our first dog, but it turned out that the dog would be the one doing the choosing. The shelter had picked up three puppies that had been left on the side of the highway. Just as my husband and I were sizing them up, one stumbled over to me and licked my toes, which were sticking out of my sandals. I fell in love with her, took her home and named her Tobi. I've always wondered what perils poor Tobi had been through before being picked up, but I know that she has had a good life ever since. And she's still licking my toes.

—BARBARA LAVALETTE
RALEIGH, NORTH CAROLINA
🐕 TOBI, MIXED BREED, 6

I WAS VISITING MY COUSIN IN THE SOUTH BRONX, and from her balcony I saw a dog wandering around on the street. I went downstairs and called her over, but she was timid. Eventually she came over and I took her upstairs but didn't plan on keeping her. I've been known to pick up strays and find homes for them; that was the plan this time too. But at the last minute, I decided to keep her. I named her Roxy Bronx. The way I see it, we found each other. She was meant to come and live with me. She is a great companion, and I'm blessed to have her.

> —SHARON TOOMER
> BROOKLYN, NEW YORK
> 🐕 ROXY BRONX, MIXED BREED, 5

• • • • • • • •

I WAS AT THE MOVIES WITH MY WIFE. We had to wait in line in the rain. A Doberman came strolling up the street. Everyone else was afraid of the dog, but my wife, the animal lover she is, went up to it, against my better judgment. She put the dog in our car. When we came out of the movie, the dog was sleeping in the back seat. We stopped at the grocery store on the way home and got some dog food; you could tell the dog had been on the street for a while because he ate all of the food. The next day we put an ad in the paper and no one answered it. The next thing I knew, I was the owner of a Doberman named Buddy.

> —BARRY
> LOS ANGELES, CALIFORNIA
> 🐕 BUDDY, DOBERMAN, 3

> *My friends adopted a stray they found playing in traffic. They named him Foolish.*
>
> —N.
> BROOKLYN, NEW YORK
> 🐕 FOOLISH, 10, MIXED BREED

WE PICKED UP OUR SEVEN-MONTH-OLD PUP and prepared for the one-hour ride home. Within two minutes she threw up inside the car, and again twice more. The whining was incessant; she could not be held, would not stay in her carrying case, and absolutely could not calm down. Classical music did not help. My husband, who after much urging had agreed to get a dog, looked at me with the worst, "I told you so" eyes and we rode home in silence, between whines.

—JENNIFER KRAMER
MINNEAPOLIS, MINNESOTA
🐕 LUCILLE BELLE, 1

Smart Dog

How smart is your dog? Sure, he comes when you call; maybe he even sits, stays, and rolls over ... sometimes. But can your dog pick locks? Get you a beer out of the refrigerator? Tell time? Go to the bathroom—in the bathroom—when Nature calls? In this chapter, you'll meet some really high-IQ canines. Just don't tell your dog about these genius achievements; you'll risk giving him an inferiority complex.

ONE DAY WHEN MY MOTHER was coming over for a visit, I told my dog, "Hey Bear, RoRo's coming over." I was shocked when he went straight over to the door and sat down, waiting for her (or someone) to arrive. I thought it must have been a strange coincidence, but then later that day, as I told my husband the story, I said the same thing and he again went straight to the door and sat down. We now tell Bear in advance when anyone will be visiting and he always waits by the front door to greet them!

—GRETCHEN FROEHLICH
CINCINNATI, OHIO
BEAR, GERMAN SHEPHERD, 4

MY SISTER-IN-LAW CAME OVER a couple of years ago with her little baby. I was setting up for a garage sale and the baby was getting fussy, so she decided to take him on a walk in his stroller. The baby was amused by our dog, Kirbie, so my sister-in-law asked if she could take him along. It seemed to start out fine, but a while later I see my sister-in-law coming up the street, huffing and puffing, the baby on her hip and Kirbie sitting in the stroller like he was king of the world. You've got to hand it to our dog; he's no dummy.

—ALICE OLSON
STILLWATER, MINNESOTA
KIRBIE, YORKSHIRE TERRIER, 5

MY DOG'S NICKNAME IS PIGLET, for good reason; she knows how to get a treat. She once came up to me and barked to let me know she had to go outside, and when I let her out she did a fake squat, ran inside, and went to the treat cupboard! Yes, my dog tried to fake a pee for a treat!

—DEBBI SCHWARTZENFELD
BERKLEY, MICHIGAN
🐕 KALLI, 5

. . . .

MAXI HAS A METAL BOWL. In the summer, I freeze water in it for him to lick. When the bowl is empty, he clicks on it with his nails. We can hear the "tap, tap, tap" all around the house. It is his way of saying, "I'm out of water here."

—DIANA
THE BRONX, NEW YORK
🐕 MAXIMILLION, MIXED BREED, 10

. . . .

COOPER MONSTER MILLER IS A MALE BOUVIER des Flandres. He's not the sharpest tool in the shed, but his IQ is directly related to the volume of human food that he can find a way to get to. Example: Cooper can open the refrigerator door with his paws. Given that he stands on his hind legs at about 5'5", he has figured out that he can open the freezer as well.

—DAWN
VENICE, CALIFORNIA
🐕 COOPER MONSTER MILLER, 3

ROSCOE LOVED TO PLAY with a tennis ball. I would often hide the ball behind my back or switch it between my hands as he jumped and ran around me looking for it. One day I hid the ball by lying on top of it and Roscoe didn't quite know what to make of it. I eventually showed him where it was hidden and we continued our game. After that, he began hiding the ball from me by lying down and tucking it under his chin and chest.

—ROSEMARY SUSZYNSKI
NORTH TONAWANDA, NEW YORK
🐕 ROSCOE, 9

Buster can open a locked door. He scratches at the door as if to knock and then jiggles it open.

*—NIKI FRIEDMAN
NEW YORK,
NEW YORK
🐕 BUSTER, 4*

SUNNY LEARNED TO HELP HERSELF to the refrigerator. She was once a stray and even though she has become part of a loving and secure home, she never passes up a free meal! She watched her mom and dad take good things to eat out of that big white box in the kitchen, so she learned to do it herself. However, she's never learned to close the door when she was done or clean up the mess she made.

—DENISE FLECK
SHADOW HILLS, CALIFORNIA
🐕 SUNNY, YELLOW LABRADOR RETRIEVER, 10
🐕 DUCHESS, SHETLAND-SHEEPDOG MIX, 16
🐕 RICO, LABRADOR RETRIEVER, 11
🐕 REX, AKITA-BORDER COLLIE MIX, 11
🐕 HAIKU, LONG COATED JAPANESE AKITA, 1

MY HUSBAND BEN GOT OUR DOG, Molly, when he was
at college. She went to all of his classes with him, and
actually marched in graduation with him—he had her on
a leash when he got his diploma.

—KATHLEEN SOLOMON
WASHINGTON, D.C.
🐕 MOLLY, BEARDED COLLIE, 12

Tippy figured out on his own how to use
the bathroom. He would go into the shower
stall to relieve himself when we were
unavailable to take him out.

—MILLIE
HARTSDALE, NEW YORK
🐕 TIPPY, ITALIAN GREYHOUND, 10

OUR GOLDEN RETRIEVER CAN TELL TIME. At 4:45 every
evening, he goes into the kitchen and barks for dinner.
He barks, but waits until 5:00, when he knows he's
supposed to eat.

—NICK
NEW CITY, NEW YORK
🐕 BOOMER, GOLDEN RETRIEVER, 8

BLUE'S BREWS

My blue heeler, Poodnah, is one of the most intelligent dogs I've ever seen. She quickly learned many tricks: playing dead; catching a Frisbee; fetching television remotes on demand; climbing up ladders; getting her own biscuits out of the box when told to do so; and many others. Most of all, she loves her toys, which she can fetch on command by their names. One day I had a college friend over to watch a basketball game. I had my friend tell her to get her toys by name, and one by one she would bring them to him. I decided to cap off the show with a new trick I had taught her just the day before. I told him to ask the dog to get him a beer. As planned, Poodnah immediately went to the kitchen and, with the help of a dishtowel tied to the handle, opened the refrigerator. We could hear her moving the cans around, and then she came trotting back into the living room with a can of beer in her mouth. The trick was working perfectly. But instead of giving the can to my friend, she continued past his chair and went over to her dog bed and began chewing the sides of the can. Now tell me that isn't the smartest dog—she knew the importance of a cold beer at game time!

—SHAWN CONNORS
CINCINNATI, OHIO
🐕 BO, BLACK LABRADOR, 6
🐕 POODNAH, AUSTRALIAN CATTLE DOG, 5

ANNIE WAS QUITE SMART and did some pretty amazing things. If we told her to go downstairs and wake up our son Brad, she would go down the steps and run straight into his room and jump on his bed. When she came up, we would tell her to go down and wake up our other son, Wes. She'd then go down the steps and take a left to go to Wes's room. Sometimes she would come back up too quickly and we knew that she hadn't jumped on his bed. Then we would ask her if she got Wes up and she would look a bit sheepish and we would tell her to go get Wes up again. She'd go downstairs, take a left, and not come back up for awhile. I knew that she had completed her job and was up on Wes's bed, staring at him and breathing on him to wake him up.

—CINDY SCHWIE
ROSEVILLE, MINNESOTA
🐕 DUFFER, 15 🐕 ANNIE, 15, MIXED BREEDS

• • • • • • • • •

Among **ANNIE'S** household chores: waking up the children each morning, on command.

CINDY SCHWIE (OWNER)
ROSEVILLE, MINNESOTA

TIPPY, an Italian Greyhound, relieves himself in the shower stall when his parents aren't home.

MILLIE (OWNER)
HARTSDALE, NEW YORK

WE LEAVE OUR BEDROOM DOOR CLOSED at night because if we leave it open, Hailey sometimes has accidents around the apartment. So, when she wants to wake us up in the middle of the night in order to go to the bathroom, she will hit the door stopper on the back of the door. It makes this loud "boinngg" noise. She will hit it, and then look up at you to see if you are getting up. If you haven't gotten up, she will hit it again and again, faster and faster, until we get up. And of course, we get up!

> —HEATHER NELSON
> PLYMOUTH, MINNESOTA
> 🐕 HAILEY, MIXED BREED, 1

· · · · · · · · ·

CASEY AND I HAVE A MORNING RITUAL. She claws me awake when she needs to be taken out to pee, and I ignore her until the clawing/dog breath combination gets unbearable. One morning I must have been extra tired, because I was doing a stellar job of ignoring her. She was clawing, and I was sleeping through it, until a weird noise came to my ears. I opened one eye and saw that she had given up on me and started clawing at my alarm clock, alternating with staring at me hopefully.

> —SHAROLYN WIEBE
> VANCOUVER, CANADA
> 🐕 CASEY, SHELTIE, 9

MY DOG PLAYS HIS OWN GAME of hide-and-seek. He takes his ball and puts it on the center of his blanket. Then he takes each corner of the blanket in his mouth and folds it over the ball until the ball is hidden. He then tries to get the ball out, but not in the same thoughtful way he buried it. His little game keeps him busy for long periods of time.

—JULIE
BEVERLY HILLS, CALIFORNIA
🐾 MAX, SHIH TZU-POODLE MIX, 4

• • • • • • • • •

WHEN MY HUSBAND AND I were college students, we decided it would be best to leave our dog Aquarius in the basement while we were in class. As soon as we'd get home, we'd run downstairs to find him lying on the basement floor, just like an angel. So why was the door from the basement to the house open? It wasn't long before it became obvious that Aquarius had learned how to open the door, spend his days upstairs, and then head back to the basement as soon as he heard the garage door open. The only thing he hadn't figured out how to do was to get the door closed again. We finally decided that any dog smart enough to escape and then return to his post should have the run of the house—so Aquarius was out of the basement for good.

—CONNIE THROOP
ST. LOUIS, MISSOURI
🐾 AQUARIUS, LABRADOR MIX
🐾 PRINCESSA, MIXED BREED

TRUCK. STOP.

Our house was on Route 25, a fairly busy (for a small town in Maine) east-west road. Maggie, a shelter dog, always appeared to be afraid of the leash, so we used one as little as possible. We always simply opened the door and let Maggie out. She would wander into the fields behind the house to do what she had to do, then return and sit on the porch until we let her back in. One day, I went out to look for her in the field and couldn't find her. Then I saw her walking along the road on the other side of the street. I started to panic; tractor-trailers often came by with a lot of speed and rarely slowed down. But I would not holler to Maggie to "stay"; a man I know once did just that with his dog, and when the dog heard his voice, she ran to him and was hit by a car. I was forced to watch, and trust. Maggie walked along slowly until she was directly across from the house. Then, as a speeding tractor-trailer barreled down the road, she sat down and waited! When the truck, and the backed-up traffic behind it, passed, she got up and casually walked across the street to the house.

—Bill Whelan
Freeport, Maine
🐕 Maggie, Collie mix, 14
🐕 Buttone, Dalmatian, 4
🐕 Sam, Lhasa Apso-Poodle, 14

This Shetland-Sheepdog mix named DUCHESS is fond of her bed.

DENISE FLECK (OWNER)
SHADOW HILLS, CALIFORNIA

CHARLOTTE HAS GREAT MAMA-DOG RECOGNITION. She was bred by a friend of mine who still has her mom and some other dogs. Every morning we all go for walks together, and as soon as Charlotte smells her mom (she doesn't even see her yet), she starts going crazy. She pulls on me, her body shakes, and her tail wags frantically. I think it's amazing that at four years old, she still knows her mom.

——VERONICA BARKER
TUSTIN, CALIFORNIA
🐕 CHARLOTTE, ENGLISH SPRINGER SPANIEL, 3
🐕 NICK, MIXED BREED, 12

. . . .

MISTY HAS FOUND THE VALUE OF A CHAIR. She knows that she can move a chair, hop up on it and get anything she needs. She moves it so she can get a toy. She'll move it to get papers, food, or whatever else she wants to help her get through her day.

——IAN LONG
RANCHO SANTA MARGARITA, CALIFORNIA
🐕 MISTY, 3 🐕 BRANDI, 1, SHELTIES

. . . .

BOXERS ARE REALLY INTELLIGENT DOGS; I have a neighbor with a boxer who can open the fridge. Our dog, Louie, has a really big vocabulary: He knows all his toys names, and if I tell him to go get a drink, he does.

——LESLIE
MINNEAPOLIS, MINNESOTA
🐕 LOUIE, BOXER-ENGLISH SPRINGER SPANIEL MIX, 3

MY DOG IS THE BEST RUNNING PARTNER in the world. When we run together and we come to a street to cross, he'll sit down and wait for me to get there and make sure cars aren't coming before we cross together. He'll always make sure that he's between me and a stranger, a new dog, or a car. He always protects me.

—ANDREA WIESE
CHESTERTON, INDIANA
🐕 JACKSON, MIXED BREED, 4

* * * * * * * *

NICK HAS THE HUGEST VOCABULARY you've ever seen in your life. I can say, "Let's go up to the office." I can say, "Let's go to the sewing room," or "Let's go down to the garage," and he goes. When I talk to him he truly pays attention. He really has a huge comprehension about what's going on around him.

—VERONICA BARKER
TUSTIN, CALIFORNIA
🐕 CHARLOTTE, ENGLISH SPRINGER SPANIEL, 3
🐕 NICK, MIXED BREED, 12

Dumb Dog, Crazy Dog

On the other hand, some dogs aren't all that bright. And some are, well, crazy. There are the barkers, the biters, and the chasers; the plush-obsessed and the postman-obsessed; the fixated and the fixed. We strive to understand their behavior, even when there's no good explanation. ("Oh, Ruby just wanted to see what was on the other side of the glass cabinet … ") But no matter how dumb they act, or how inexplicable their actions, we love them, right?

I HAD GOTTEN MY DOG a big water dish, maybe 12 inches wide, with a dispenser bottle attached. One morning, about 2 a.m., I woke up to a loud racket. Gus was backing in through his doggy door, the water bottle between his teeth, banging the bowl from side to side because it was too wide to fit through the doggy door. He did manage to get it inside.

—MARIA
SOUTH BRUNSWICK, NEW JERSEY
MAGGIE, 8 GUS, 2

McNab, my mother-in-law's dog, would bark incessantly at a square of parquet flooring that made a clicking noise whenever someone stepped on it.

—N.
BROOKLYN, NEW YORK

MY SISTER'S DOG, SCOOBY, is a big, friendly, black Labrador. One summer, my sister hosted a party at her house and rented an inflatable bounce house for the guests. Scooby, of course, wanted to get right into the bounce house and play, but he knew he wasn't allowed and behaved himself most of the day. He behaved himself until the party was over and he found himself in the yard all alone with the bounce house. I was cleaning up in the kitchen and saw him out the window. He looked to the right and then looked to the left. When he thought no one was watching, he made a bee-line to the bounce house and bounded right inside. He had so much fun running around in there that the only way to get him out was to drag him by his collar.

—JENNIFER
LOCKPORT, NEW YORK
SCOOBY, LABRADOR, 4
SHEEPDOG, 1

MY DOG BITES EVERYTHING: carpets, shoes, curtains, toes. While on a walk one day, he ran from me towards the front of a moving car, thinking he could bite the hood. He ended up getting run over. He recovered, but after that he refused to stand near a car, even if it was parked.

—RUBEN REEVES
CHICAGO, ILLINOIS
🐕 SHANG, MIXED BREED, 2

SMITHERS, OUR RESCUED RACING GREYHOUND, had spent his life going only from kennel to racetrack, and back. So when we got him, he didn't know how to live in our world. He walked into doors. We had to teach him to go up and down stairs.

—MEG
MONTCLAIR, NEW JERSEY
🐕 SMITHERS, GREYHOUND, 3

TOBY, MY LAB, IS OBSESSED WITH WATER. If there is a body of water, she has to jump in it. If there is a bowl of water, she tries to jump in that, too. The problem is, she weighs over 50 pounds. Whenever we go to the dog park, the first thing she does is check out each bowl of water. She takes her front paws, places them in the bowl and starts frantically moving her paws as if she's digging. She does this until all of the bowls are completely emptied.

—ANONYMOUS
AGOURA HILLS, CALIFORNIA
🐕 TOBY, LABRADOR, 4

BARNABAS BARKS AT THE WIND, a habit he picked up from Maggie, the dog I grew up with. Before we started to bring Barnabas over to my mom and dad's house, he never barked at the wind. But once he saw Maggie doing it nonstop, it was "doggie see, doggie do." Thanks for the legacy, Maggie!

—CLARE DAVIS
MINNEAPOLIS, MINNESOTA
🐕 BARNABAS, MIXED BREED, 6

Our dog would go around to other houses and bring back their newspapers. He would steal our neighbors' shoes from outside their front doors.

— MYRA BRAVO
SAN ANTONIO,
TEXAS
🐕 *GOLDEN*
RETRIEVER, 2

I LOVE TO WINDSURF and would often take Buddy to the beach with me. He would never go in the water, though. It was the weirdest thing, because he seemed to want to take that leap into the ocean and be right there with me, but he just couldn't get over the hump. Instead, he would race back and forth along the shoreline, following my windsurfer each time I changed direction.

—BARRY
LOS ANGELES, CALIFORNIA
🐕 BUDDY, DOBERMAN, 3

MY DOG IS SO DUMB that when he played fetch, if the ball rolled under a car he wouldn't stop. He'd just ram his head into the side of the car and, once, a parked garbage truck.

—JOHN FOCKE
MARQUETTE, MICHIGAN
🐕 JED, MIXED BREED, 12

I USED TO KISS MY DOG on the mouth until I found out what she eats around the house when I'm not looking. For example, she likes to eat tissue after you have just blown your nose.

—EVETTE WILLIS
CHICAGO, ILLINOIS
JAZZY, LHASA APSO, 1

* * * * * * * *

CLIFTON was adopted from a shelter as a puppy in Atlanta, Georgia.

J.A. (OWNER)

* * * * * * * *

OUR DOG WILL RETRIEVE ROCKS FROM A LAKE. If someone (usually a child) throws a rock, she will dunk her head into the water and retrieve the same rock. One problem is that rocks are tough on teeth, especially if the dog tries to catch them (which ours does, of course). Aleria has broken both of her lower canine teeth because of this habit.

—TIM POWELL
OAKDALE, MINNESOTA
ALERIA, MIXED BREED, 9

PREVENTIVE INSANITY

We got Clifton at the shelter when she was a puppy. One sign that she wasn't treated well is her reaction to any medium-sized, stick-like tool—wooden spoon, flyswatter, etc. If you hold one, she runs to a corner and hides. It has gotten to the point where she'll hear a fly buzzing around, and she'll do everything she can to eat the fly, just to keep you from breaking out the swatter. This goes for bees and other stinging insects, too. She will actually swallow a bee—and it clearly stings her, judging by her reaction—before she'll have you break out that fly swatter. She also happens to be an alpha dog; she's aggressive with any other dog that we've had. It's as if she's worried that the other dog is going to act up at certain moments (forcing the owners to break out the swatter), and so she attacks that dog to get them in line. For instance, we used to have an epileptic Aussie. This was loads of fun—one crazy dog and one sick dog. And when the sick dog would fall into a grand mal seizure, Clifton would do everything in her power to get to him so she could attack him. Survival of the fittest, you see. On the upside, she's like our house alarm: If a leaf falls from a neighbor's tree down the street, she's barking to let everyone know.

—J.A.
ATLANTA, GEORGIA
🐕 SOPHIE, LABRADOR-AUSTRALIAN SHEPHERD MIX, 2
🐕 CLIFTON, MIXED BREED, 10

LABS ARE KNOWN TO BE CHEWERS. When Snickers was a couple of years old, she grabbed a needle and thread out of my hand and swallowed it. I called the vet. He told me I had to wait a couple of days to see if she passed it. So we waited, and no luck. She had to have surgery. The vet called a few hours after it was over. "I want you to know Snickers is doing well," he said. "We got the needle. But what was the pink and white material?" That was from the kitchen chair. "What was the white paper?" That was a Post-It note. "What was the eraser?" One of the kid's toys. So, she was all cleaned out.

—YVONNE
CHERRY HILL, NEW JERSEY
SNICKERS, 11   MAX, 3

Some dogs chase cars, but my dog chases airplanes. Every time a jet flies over our house, she chases it from one end of the yard to the other, barking ferociously.

—C.A.
CINCINNATI, OHIO
SYDNEY, SHEPHERD MIX, 8

WHEN MY HUSBAND WAS COURTING ME, our dog Jill used to set herself between us on the couch and growl at him if he got too close. He tried everything to get her to move, but nothing worked; nothing, that is, until he accidentally discovered Jill's love of popsicles. If he offered Jill a popsicle, she'd hop down off the couch, hold the popsicle between her front paws and eat it on the floor. And for however long that took, my future husband could get next to me on the couch without interference.

—PAT
ROSEVILLE, MINNESOTA
🐕 JILL, GERMAN SHEPHERD, 5
🐕 PUPPY, 3 🐕 MAGGIE, 11, MIXED BREEDS

MUSHU AND TAG HAVE A FAVORITE ACTIVITY. They go to work with me every day and as soon as we get to work their favorite thing is to look for the woman in the accounting department. She always has treats for them and they literally race to her desk. When she's not there, they sort of sigh and mope, but as soon as she walks in the door they go wild and crazy and chase after her. Mushu makes lots of noises right in the middle of the office. When they finally get their treat the first thing they do is to find me so they can let me know that they've had their treat. Then they settle in for the day.

—GENEVIEVE YATES
CAPE TOWN, SOUTH AFRICA
🐕 TAG, COCKER SPANIEL, 10
🐕 MUSHU, SHIH TZU, 3

CASEROLE DE LAPIN

ONE TIME OUR DOG CAUGHT A RABBIT AND KILLED IT. But that's not the dumb part; she started eating it! The whole back end of the rabbit was gone when I found her. I know that's what carnivores do; kill animals and eat them. *But I feed you! You dumb dog!*

—TIM POWELL
OAKDALE, MINNESOTA
🐕 ALERIA, MIXED BREED, 9

• • • • • • • • •

MY WIFE, JACKIE, went outside to let the dog in, and she came back inside screaming, "You have to go outside. You're not going to believe it." The dog had caught a rabbit and had eaten the carcass from the back end all the way to the midsection. The only thing left of the rabbit was the waist to the top of the head. When our dog saw me, he was startled, so he stood up. He had the rabbit carcass on his head, like a hat.

—DAVE BARTOK
UNION, NEW JERSEY
🐕 PUPALUP, 17
🐕 CUJO, MIXED BREED, 1

HYDROPHOBIA

Casey hates water. I don't understand why, but water is pretty much the worst thing in the world, according to her. When we walk, she prances around the puddles. Bathing? We may as well be beating her. I didn't really understand the true extent of her water hatred, however, until one morning when she woke me up to be taken out. I stumbled out of bed, threw clothes on and took her outside ... only to have her stop dead when she realized it was raining. Five minutes ago this dog was swearing up, down, and sideways that she needed to pee immediately or disaster would result. Now she was standing on my front porch, looking at the rain while I stood halfway down the steps (being rained on, I might add) trying to pull her down the stairs. She won, and I went back to bed. Her hatred of water does have a limit, though. One night when my husband was chopping carrots, a piece fell into her water dish. She sat there for five minutes trying to figure out if the carrot was worth getting her snout wet. She would dip her nose in, then jump back ... dip in, jump back ... finally she went for it. And after eating the carrot, Casey spent the next 10 minutes running around the house wiping her nose on everything she could find.

—SHAROLYN WIEBE
VANCOUVER, CANADA
🐕 CASEY, SHELTIE, 9

BARNABAS, a mixed breed, barks at the wind and chases the same squirrel around a tree every night.

CLARE DAVIS (OWNER)
MINNEAPOLIS, MINNESOTA

GOING POSTAL

I OFTEN WONDER IF THE DEEP-SEATED HATRED for mailmen is bred into dogs. Our dog is the most easygoing dog you will ever run across. He wouldn't say boo to a ghost—except when the mailman shows up. He goes crazy every day, jumping up and down and barking. It's inexplicable. Our mailman is a very nice guy, too. He brings treats for the dog once in a while. I wonder if it's just that blue uniform that sets dogs off. One day I'm going to ask the mailman to come to our house on his day off to see if the dog would react the same way if he wears jeans and a T-shirt.

—MICHAEL CONWAY
HARRISONBURG, VIRGINIA
🐕 8

• • • • • • • • •

OUR DOG HAS A HATRED FOR DELIVERY PEOPLE. I work out of the home and get a daily package from UPS. Every day the deliveryman would come and the dog would lose her mind. We noticed that it didn't happen so often with the mailman, but the UPS guy would always set her off. The vet told us that sometimes the way certain people walk can remind dogs of someone else in their life that they may have had a bad experience with.

—MARK MATSON
DRY RIDGE, KENTUCKY
🐕 5

THE MAILMAN IS MY DOG'S OBSESSION. He carved a path of dead grass in the front yard from running back and forth after the mailman, who wound up macing our dog and ceasing to deliver our mail. He left us a note saying, "If you want your mail, move your dog out of my path." The dog is in the backyard now.

—MARCOS DE LA CRUZ
SAN ANTONIO, TEXAS
🐕 CHIHUAHUA, 5

IF STANLEY WAS OUTSIDE when our mailman, Clarence, came by, he would not only follow him, but actually escort him for the rest of his route. Mind you, Stanley walked with him, not behind him. When Clarence finished his route, he would accompany Stanley back to our house. This happened several times each week. This routine continued until Clarence retired.

—RAY
FLORISSANT, MISSOURI
🐕 STANLEY, COCKER SPANIEL-GOLDEN RETRIEVER MIX, 13

BARKLY LOVES TO CHASE SMALL ANIMALS. At first we thought it was funny. We would get a kick watching him go after roaches, flies, mosquitoes, and moths. It stopped being funny when his fetish turned from bugs to rodents. I was in my kitchen one day and Barkly came through his dog door with some fur hanging from his mouth. I thought it was just a toy but it turned out to be a rat. It was the most disgusting thing I've ever seen.

—KRISTI
LOS ANGELES, CALIFORNIA
🐕 BARKLY, JACK RUSSELL, 4

• • • • • • • •

PUMPKIN, A MINIATURE DACHSUND, was obsessed with water bottles. She'd sit next to you and stare at you if you were drinking one, or sit at your feet and not stop barking until you gave it to her. Then she'd hold the bottle down with her paw and twist off the cap with her teeth. Once she got the cap off, she wanted nothing to do with it. She was also obsessive about pizza crusts or egg rolls from Chinese restaurants. My dad would give one to her, and she'd wrap it in a blanket and protect it, growling at anyone who tried to take it away. After about a week, we'd have to go down at night when she was asleep or when she wasn't guarding her prized possessions, find them, and throw them away!

—TISHA
BOSTON, MASSACHUSETTS
🐕 PUMPKIN, MINIATURE DASCHUND, 9

COBBER IS TOTALLY OBSESSED with plush squeaky toys. There isn't a toy in existence that doesn't stop him in his tracks, unless it's one of his old toys. He's like a child who quickly gets sick of what he has, and only likes something new. I first knew we had a problem when we went to a friend's house and Cobber stole their dog's toys. Not only did he steal them; when their rightful owner tried to get them back, he growled. Don't mess with Cobber and his toys!

—LINDA KORBEL
CULVER CITY, CALIFORNIA
🐕 A.J., 12, 🐕 ADDIE, 12, GOLDEN RETRIEVERS
🐕 COBBER, LABRADOODLE, 16

• • • • • • • • •

OUR DOG GOES CRAZY ANYTIME he sees one of those red laser light pointers that people use in presentations. Our kids got hold of one of those once at a birthday party in our basement and they literally had Reilly running for a couple of hours chasing the light all over the basement. I heard all the screaming and yelling and laughing and Reilly barking and just assumed it was the typical kids behavior at a birthday party. But when I went downstairs with the cake I saw Reilly passed out on the floor. He was just beat.

—DERRITH MURPHY
BABENHAUSEN, GERMANY
🐕 REILLY, 1

CRAZY DOGS: A KID'S-EYE VIEW

WHEN WE LET DARBY INSIDE he goes crazy and runs as fast as the speed of light. My mom yells, "Darby alert!" and we have to get out of his way.

> —COLE DRAPER
> DALLAS, TEXAS
> 🐕 CASEY, GOLDEN RETRIEVER, 13
> 🐕 DARBY, LABRADOR-POODLE MIX, 3

WHEN WE CLAP OUR HANDS AND SAY "cha, cha, cha," our dog runs around our backyard and we laugh.

> —SOPHIE ALFORD
> DALLAS, TEXAS

MY DOG LUCKY WAS SO OVERPROTECTIVE of my little brother that he didn't want any other human coming in physical contact with him. When my sisters, my brother, and I played football in the backyard and we tackled my brother, Lucky would come in our face and bark or jump on us to get us away from him. It was like the dog didn't even know us. I knew then that dogs have favorites too.

> —CORAVIECE TERRY
> MOUNDS, ILLINOIS
> 🐕 LUCKY

WHEN SOPHIE GETS A BONE, she sort of eats it but then she buries it between the couch cushions. Clifton, our other dog, will take a few bites of her bone and leave it on the floor. Then both dogs get confused about which bone belongs to them, and we have to stop them from fighting over the bones.

—JOSEY ALLEN, 8
ATLANTA, GEORGIA
🐾 SOPHIE, 2 🐾 CLIFTON, 10

DAISY LOVES TO STEAL THINGS, and she'll bring them into her kennel. I've heard that dogs like to steal the things that smell like you. Money has a lot of people-smell on it, and Daisy will take that; or if the kids are playing cards and they put them down, she'll grab a couple and race into her kennel. She used to grab my husband's tools when he'd set them down—pliers, an Allen wrench, whatever. Whenever we can't find something we'll look in her kennel.

—SIDNEY
MINNEAPOLIS, MINNESOTA
DAISY, YORKSHIRE TERRIER, 1

* * * * * * * *

ONE TIME WHEN MY DOG WAS MAD at my mom, she took a Kleenex and put it on top of my mom's bed. She is not supposed to be on the furniture, but she wanted her to know she had been there.

—JENNA WOODY
JOHNSTON, IOWA
BRITTANY, SPANIEL, 12

* * * * * * * *

WE HAVE A POND BEHIND OUR HOUSE, and our dog Lucy used to like to watch the fish. She would just stand over them and stare. Then she would start to chase them until eventually she would lose her footing and fall right into the pond.

—JOHN
LOS ANGELES, CALIFORNIA
FRANK, WESTIE, 14
LUCY, AUSTRALIAN CATTLE DOG, 12

ONE DAY, WINNIE, MY DOG, was chasing my cat around one of the chairs in our TV room. At some point, Winnie lost track of what she was doing; the third time around she failed to notice that my cat had jumped to the top of the recliner. Winnie went round and round the chair at least three more times before she realized she was no longer chasing the cat.

—CATY CUBA
ST. LOUIS, MISSOURI
🐕 WINNIE, 6

* * * * * * * *

THE DUMBEST THING OUR DOG GRIFFEY ever did: We put him in his crate with a pillow before we left the house, and when we came back home he was buried in white fluff. He had torn up the pillow and all we could see was his little face sticking out from underneath white stuffing.

—CHAR LAVALETTE
RALEIGH, NORTH CAROLINA
🐕 GRIFFEY, BEAGLE, 8
🐕 RANDY, TERRIER MIX, 9

* * * * * * * *

MY HUSBAND SAYS OUR DOG, KIRBIE, "is a scaredy-cat, a little chicken." We will take him for a walk around the block, and if Kirbie hears a noise, like a leaf crackling, he "puts the brakes on." He will not move; he stiffens and then hides behind my husband! And as we continue to walk he does this every few feet. We end up just carrying him.

—ALICE OLSON
STILLWATER, MINNESOTA
🐕 KIRBIE, YORKSHIRE TERRIER, 5

ELMER LOVES CHASING TENNIS BALLS. The only problem is that he doesn't retrieve them. He runs to the ball and barks at it. He'll keep barking until I throw it for him again. When we arrive at the park I try to ignore him, but sure enough, Elmer finds the one tennis ball out of the hundred on the ground that is the dirtiest and most peed-on, and he barks and stares at it. I just turn my head, hoping he'll get tired and distracted. Eventually someone throws the ball for him and he's thrilled and runs after it, only to bark at it once more. I tell my wife that I'm going to get him a T-shirt that says, "Please do not throw the ball for me."

—ANONYMOUS
LOS ANGELES, CALIFORNIA
🐕 ELMER, 4 🐕 MABEL, 4, BEAGLES

Go, Dog!

Poetry in motion, or just lots of commotion? The dogs in this chapter really get a move on, with sports equipment ranging from Frisbees to dirty socks. Athletic, acrobatic, or just frenetic, some dogs enter races while others just go for coffee. And if you want to read about bike-riding, waterskiing dogs, you'll find them here.

LUCY IS THE MOST SOCIAL ANIMAL I've ever known and loves nothing more than the dog park. The second she gets in range, she bolts into a pile of dogs and remains in a wrestling match until the poor victim gets loose. Then she heads for the next group of calm canines, taking each one down. She's in complete bliss while the other parents look at us wide-eyed and nervously comment on her "energy" and "enthusiasm."

—JENNIFER KRAMER
MINNEAPOLIS, MINNESOTA
🐕 LUCILLE BELLE, 1

• • • • • • • •

I WAS IN THE KITCHEN ONE DAY, doing the dishes, and I thought my dogs were in the house. The next thing I know, Michael, my husband, brings our dog Woody in through the living room. I said, "How did you get Woody? I thought he was in the house!" Michael told me that Woody had jumped out of the house through the second-story window. Apparently he had seen a contractor coming, started barking, and the screen fell off. He didn't fall; he landed right on the ground and started to run. Thankfully, he didn't get hurt.

—LINDA SMITH
WESTLAKE VILLAGE, CALIFORNIA
🐕 WOODY, BORDER COLLIE, 5
🐕 MILLIE, ENGLISH SHEPHERD, 10

BERNESE MOUNTAIN DOGS are not known for being strong swimmers; in fact most just like to wade in the water. Well, my husband was convinced that our newest girl should be a swimmer. We took her to the river many times, and she would run into the water like gangbusters and then proceed to sink like a lead weight. This was terrible to watch because she wanted to swim; she just could not get the dog paddle down. I invested in a large orange life preserver for dogs, which we put on her every time she went swimming. To this day we cannot keep her out of the water.

—HEIDI HENDERSON
KILLINGTON, VERMONT
EMMA BLU, 1 LOGAN, 1
SHASTA DELANEY, 5, BERNESE MOUNTAIN DOGS

I WASN'T ALLOWED TO BRING LADY on a waterskiing trip because the people I was going with said it wouldn't be fair to leave her on the dock the whole time. I insisted that she would waterski with me. Instead of skis, she sat on my lap in one of those rubber doughnuts and the boat pulled us around the lake. She was always great when it came to sports.

—LISA MCKEARNEY
LOS ANGELES, CALIFORNIA
LADY, MIXED BREED, 16

KAYCEE COMPETES IN OBEDIENCE, agility and carting. A Bernese's job was to haul the milk from the farmer to the dairies. The task is now called carting, and it is a sport in which dogs compete. Kaycee was the first Bernese Mountain Dog in Southern California to earn a Working Dog/Excellent title. Dogs earn that title by having advanced titles in two other sports combined in addition to earning a type of advance obedience title.

—ROBIN WINDLINGER
FULLERTON, CALIFORNIA
🐕 KAYCEE, BERNESE MOUNTAIN DOG, 9

• • • • • • • •

ANNIE'S FAVORITE ACTIVITY was bike riding. She had her own seat on the back of my bike that she rode in. For Annie it was her time to stick her head out and let her ears fly in the wind. As she rode on the back of my bike, I sometimes thought about one of my favorite movies, "The Wizard of Oz": Annie/Toto and Cindy/Miss Gulch, cruising down Ryan Avenue. When we stopped at stop-lights, people would sometimes ask how we got her to sit in the basket that was her seat. Simple reply: She loves it!

—CINDY SCHWIE
ROSEVILLE, MINNESOTA
🐕 DUFFER, 15 🐕 ANNIE, 15, MIXED BREEDS

BENVY'S FAVORITE TOY IS A CANVAS DOLL that looks like Bill Clinton. She picks him up by the legs and thrashes him on the ground. If you try to take Bill away from her to throw it to her, she growls. She's a very cute dog, but looks so ferocious when she's playing with him. Recently, President Bush was on the TV giving a speech, and she looked to the TV and cocked her head as if she were listening. She then trotted over and got Bill Clinton and started thrashing him. I told my husband "Well, I guess our dog is a Republican."

—EMILY MASON
CINCINNATI, OHIO
🐕 BENVY, BLACK LABRADOR-CHOW CHOW MIX, 7

• • • • • • • •

CAESAR WAS HIS NAME, escaping was his game. We got him as a six-week-old bundle of Beagle. As he grew, he became the neighborhood kids' darling with his uncanny way of dodging the dogcatcher's hoop. One summer day, a large group of children chanted, "Go, Caesar, go, Caesar" as I watched Caesar lope back and forth, adroitly dodging the hoop while the dogcatchers ran behind him for 30 minutes. Finally tiring of the game, Caesar retired to his porch, while I apologized to the sweaty official and received yet another ticket for having a "dog at large."

—R.E.D.
FLORISSANT, MISSOURI
🐕 CAESAR, BEAGLE, 10

Barkley is like Air Bud. He plays basketball with my son by jumping up and trying to rebound the ball. The ball is bigger than his head!

—LAURA
LOS ANGELES,
CALIFORNIA
🐕 BARKLEY,
MINI
LABRADOODLE, 2

SPARKS LIKES TO PLAY FRISBEE. He doesn't play like other dogs, though. Most dogs chase and catch the Frisbee; Sparks picks it up from the ground and throws it, and *I* catch it. I have no idea how he learned to do this.

—CHIP MASON
LOS ANGELES, CALIFORNIA
SPARKS, GOLDEN RETRIEVER, 6

Our dog loves to take a racquet ball in his mouth, drop it, slap it with his paw, and then chase it up and down the room for hours on end. And I mean hours!

—JOHN FOCKE
MARQUETTE, MICHIGAN
JED, MIXED BREED, 12

BODI AND HUNTER LOVE TO SWIM. We have swim parties, and one time we had eighteen dogs in the pool at once. It's so fun and funny because all the dogs that come over to party bring their own toys and none of the dogs take any other dog's toy.

—SUSIE BROWN
FILLMORE, CALIFORNIA
HUNTER, 3   BODIE, 1, SHELTIES

KETZI HAS SO MUCH ENERGY. When I come home from work she literally does figure eights around my entire condo. Because she has so much energy I entered her in a dog show specifically for mutts called Nuts for Mutts. The dogs compete in categories such as most beautiful, fastest eater, most obedient, best ears, and so forth. The first time Ketzi entered, she won the award for highest jumper. Well, none of the other dogs that entered showed up. I don't care though; she won, and we have the ribbon to show for it!

—MARLA
LOS ANGELES, CALIFORNIA
🐕 KETZI, POODLE-MALTESE MIX, 6

GRETA, a four-year-old Pug, has a rival in a squirrel named Edgar.

JENNIFER KUSHNER (OWNER)
BETHLEHEM, PENNSYLVANIA

WE ONCE TOOK RUBY to one of my son's soccer games. In the middle of the game, she got loose from her leash and went completely haywire, tearing onto the field, running madly in circles, creating chaos beyond her best dreams. All the kids were screaming and the parents were jumping up, trying to figure out what was going on. The more the crowd yelled, the more she went into Lucille Ball mode, darting and dashing and spinning; she loves the attention. For the grand finale, my husband had to take a flying leap and tackle her to bring her to the ground.

—BONNIE SOLLOG
FLORAL PARK, NEW YORK
🐕 RUBY, STANDARD POODLE

· · · · · · · · ·

MY DOG PLAYS DRUMS. I'm a drummer and when she was a pup, she would listen to my band practice. One day, my guitarist came over to work with me. Ma-Buku was in the rehearsal room playing with a rubber toy that squeaked. We started to practice quietly when I heard this squeaking sound on the beat. I kid you not, Ma-Buku had picked up the beat. I looked at the guitarist and said, "I guess you don't need me anymore. The dog's got the gig down."

—JOSH C. MOSCOV
LOS ANGELES, CALIFORNIA
🐕 MA-BUKU, CHIHUAHUA, 5

MA-BUKU, a five-year-old Chihuahua, likes to play drums.

My dog plays soccer. She's a great defender; she won't let the ball go by. She'll use her nose and hit it back to me.

—GAVIN BODKIN
BRADFORD,
NEW HAMPSHIRE
🐕 *SCOTTISH*
TERRIER

WYLIE OBSESSES OVER HIS BASKETBALL. He has a regulation-size basketball and as soon as he sees it he runs over to it and barks nonstop until someone throws or kicks it for him. He knows that if he barks long enough one of us will kick it for him. He's got us trained pretty well.

—CHRISTY CONN
THOUSAND OAKS, CALIFORNIA
🐕 KATY, 1 🐕 WYLIE, 4, SHELTIES

• • • • • • • •

TRACY CONSIDERED HERSELF a great athlete. She always had one tennis ball in her mouth and another that she would play soccer with. She would run around the house kicking the ball from paw to paw, and while doing this she would also have her other ball placed safely in her mouth.

—MALCOLM
LOS ANGELES, CALIFORNIA
🐕 CINDY, 7 🐕 TRACY, 10, BOXERS

• • • • • • • •

BECAUSE I WAS AN ONLY CHILD, my dog Heather was my constant companion growing up. Just like many brothers and sisters, our favorite game was hide-and-seek. I would put her in her kennel without latching it, and then run off and hide somewhere in the house with a treat. Once I was hidden I'd call to her, and she'd come looking for me. My mother got a kick out of watching her run around the house and check my usual hiding places.

—BETH STURGEON
CHICAGO, MISSOURI
🐕 HEATHER

WALRUS IS VERY FAST, especially for a Yorkie. She chases birds at the beach. Since they all hang out in flocks, she'll run alongside them until they fly away. As soon as they settle she chases them again. She can do this for hours and we can tell these are her happiest moments.

—AMY HUANG
SANTA MONICA, CALIFORNIA
🐕 WALRUS, YORKIE, 2

Boomer's energetic jaws have consumed aerosol cans, parts of our redwood deck, pieces of concrete, patio chairs, piñon wood, razors and razor blades, and my dental mouth guard.

—TED RINEY
DALLAS, TEXAS
🐕 BOOMER, GOLDEN RETRIEVER, 2

DUFFER WAS THE BEST DARN WAGON RIDER on the block. When our sons, Brad and Wes, were young they would put Duffer in the red wagon and tie it to the back of their bikes. Duffer could often be seen soaring down the street behind one of their bikes. He loved every second of it.

—CINDY SCHWIE
ROSEVILLE, MINNESOTA
🐕 DUFFER, 15 🐕 ANNIE, 15, MIXED BREEDS

SPEX IS A HERDER. I bought him a bunch of stuffed sheep because he needed something to herd and I didn't want him to herd my other animals. He probably has about 30 stuffed animals in his kennel. Every day he takes all of his animals and spreads them throughout the house; every night we gather them up. He does the same thing the next morning.

—JOAN BALLON
LOS ANGELES, CALIFORNIA
🐾 MAGGIE, 14 🐾 SAM, 13, BRITTANY SPANIELS
🐾 SPEX, AUSTRALIAN SHEPHERD, 2

MY DOG DID NOT WIN A CONTEST, but she did enter a few fun games at the Mutts on the Mountain dog day. There was a race in which two dogs would be teamed up and they would race down a long, fenced-in stretch against each other. Someone would hold each dog at the start and the owners would go to the end and encourage the dogs to run to them. My Bernese Mountain Dog, Logan, was set to race our friend's Yellow Lab, Budweiser. At the start they both took off, but about halfway down the stretch, Logan realized that she had been separated from Bud and instantly turned back around in order to be by his side. Needless to say, she did not win, but it was true love at the finish!

—HEIDI HENDERSON
KILLINGTON, VERMONT
🐾 EMMA BLU, 1 🐾 LOGAN, 1
🐾 SHASTA DELANEY, 5, BERNESE MOUNTAIN DOGS

RUBY IS A WHITE STANDARD POODLE. She's like a cartoon French dog, with her nose in the air, walking on her tip-toes. She likes to be the center of attention and she's used to being the only dog. Sometimes my son brings his Daschund, Billy, to our summer house in Cape Cod. He's about 12 pounds and has those stubby little legs. One day we took them to a doggie beach. Billy had to keep his lead on because the first time we brought him he beelined for the ocean and started swimming toward Boston. This time, I heard people laughing and screaming. I looked around, and there's Ruby with the lead in her mouth, trotting down the beach, dragging this sack of fur through the sand. Ruby would be just as happy if Billy weren't around, but when he is, she's going to show him who's in charge.

—BONNIE SOLLOG
FLORAL PARK, NEW YORK
🐕 RUBY, STANDARD POODLE

* * * * * * * *

TUGGING IS WOODY'S THING. He will go up to you and give you his leash; he'll put it in your face until you start tugging with him. Watch out, though, because if you do it once with him, he will remember that you tugged with him once before and he will demand that you tug with him again.

—LINDA SMITH
WESTLAKE VILLAGE, CALIFORNIA
🐕 WOODY, BORDER COLLIE, 5
🐕 MILLIE, ENGLISH SHEPHERD, 10

MY PUG, GRETA, loves to chase squirrels, and squirrels seem to like egging her on. I often take her off her leash once we get to the park, and if a squirrel moves within her line of sight, she'll bark and tear after it until the squirrel finds the safety of a tree. For a while, one particular squirrel liked to come to our back door and lounge around where Greta could see him. We named the squirrel "Edgar," and now whenever my husband or I take Greta outside, we say, "Go find Edgar" and she knows it's her cue to chase squirrels.

—JENNIFER KUSHNIER
BETHLEHEM, PENNSYLVANIA
GRETA, PUG, 4
JACQUES, BRITTANY SPANIEL, 14

• • • • • • • •

GREYHOUNDS AREN'T SUPPOSED TO BARK or howl, but Smithers was a good howler. We took him to all our youth soccer games, and every time someone scored a goal, he would howl. I guess he heard the crowd cheering. Everyone loved it, and joined in. Eventually, we had to give him up for adoption. Sometime later, my husband got a message, via a chat room, that said, "Contact me. I know where Smithers is." Another soccer parent had adopted him and was bringing him to games.

—MEG
MONTCLAIR, NEW JERSEY
SMITHERS, GREYHOUND, 3

Ruby, a Standard Poodle, tends to treat canine pal Billy as if she owns him.

Bonnie Sollog (owner)
Floral Park, New York

WHENEVER LOGAN GOES OUT and about she gets a treat. People are always feeding her, and whenever we go to a café or restaurant she gets a sample of whatever we are having. One day, my husband and I were walking with Logan. At one point, we looked over, and Logan was waiting patiently in line at Starbucks. I guess Starbucks must be one of her favorite places to get treats.

—NORMA
LOS ANGELES, CALIFORNIA
🐕 LOGAN, PUG, 7
🐕 SULTAN, BOXER, 10

* * * * * * * *

CHARLOTTE IS GOING TO BE on an obedience team at the Springer Spaniel Nationals this fall. Our theme for our team is Peter Pan, so the dogs get to wear costumes. Charlotte is the only girl on the team so she is going to be Tinker Bell. She's so excited about it because she loves prissy, frilly, fluffy things. She's a princess.

—VERONICA BARKER
TUSTIN, CALIFORNIA
🐕 CHARLOTTE, ENGLISH SPRINGER SPANIEL, 3
🐕 NICK, MIXED BREED, 12

* * * * * * * *

OZZIE THINKS HE'S A SMALL DOG. But he weighs a lot, and he'll try to jump up into anyone's arms. It's the funniest thing to see this huge dog acting like he's a toy.

—CHARLENE VALDEZ
SIMI VALLEY, CALIFORNIA
🐕 OZZIE, KEESHOND, 2
🐕 DR. PEPPER, DALMATIAN, 9

MY HUSBAND AND THE DOG have started an evening ritual: he comes to bed and wrestles with her for ten minutes before either of them will go to sleep. And this is not friendly wrestling: there is fierce growling, and when she's done he's got scratches all over his arms and chest. Still, it seems to make them both happy. I think it's their way of having their own quality time, which is important so that they have a relationship, too.

—SHAROLYN WIEBE
VANCOUVER, CANADA
CASEY, SHELTIE, 9

JILL'S FAVORITE ACTIVITY WAS RUNNING in the city park, towing me behind. Once we were running in a wooded area and she leapt over a little gully. Since I did not know the gully was there, she pulled me, airborne, over the gully. Unfortunately, I hit my head on the other edge and fell into the gully. It was always exciting taking her for a walk—or, more correctly, a *run*—because you never knew if you'd make it back in one piece.

—PAT
ROSEVILLE, MINNESOTA
JILL, GERMAN SHEPHERD, 5
PUPPY, 3 MAGGIE, 11, MIXED BREEDS

EMME, A ROTTWEILER, competes in the breed ring, but in order to win in the breed ring you have to have something different than all of the other Rottweilers; she doesn't. My girl looks like the rest of them so she always takes home the third place ribbon not the first, which of course is fine with me. I guess you could say, "Always a bridesmaid, never a bride."

—JANICE
SAN DIEGO, CALIFORNIA
🐕 TOKEN, 4 🐕 DOLLY, 1, COCKER SPANIELS
🐕 EMME 🐕 BUSTER 🐕 VITA, ROTTWEILERS

• • • • • • • • •

ONCE, WHEN KYLIE CAME UPON a father and daughter at the park, she strained her leash to greet the little girl. The father politely asked if it was OK for his daughter to pet her. I said yes and the little girl was immediately covered in Kylie kisses. Then the little girl said, "Daddy, she feels like a toothbrush!" I couldn't help but laugh.

—DEBRA LEE MCAULIFFE
SAN FRANCISCO, CALIFORNIA
🐕 KYLIE, NORWICH TERRIER

Trick Dog

Once there was a man whose dog learned to play poker. He brought the dog to his regular poker game, hoping to wow his buddies. One card player at the table was unimpressed. "He's not so great," said the player. "Every time he gets a good hand, he wags his tail."

Your dog may not play poker very well, even with a royal flush in his paws. But the dogs in this chapter will give you ideas for new goals for Fido—singing, skateboarding, and furniture-surfing, just for starters. Read on.

LUCY LEARNED *SIT, DOWN*, AND *STAY* pretty quickly, so we taught her *shake* and *circle* to mix it up. She does a quick 360-degree circle and completes it so fast sometimes she hits her head on walls. Since we train before dinner, she's often so desperate for food she'll do a series of tricks—sitting, lying down, jumping up, shaking, and circling in about 10 seconds flat—no command needed.

—JENNIFER KRAMER
MINNEAPOLIS, MINNESOTA
🐾 LUCILLE BELLE, 1

Tag knows how to sneeze on command. I will say, "sneeze," and he will give a big "hachoo!"

—GENEVIEVE YATES
CAPE TOWN, SOUTH AFRICA
🐾 TAG, COCKER SPANIEL, 10
🐾 MUSHU, SHIH TZU, 3

EVERY MORNING WHEN I GET UP in the morning to use the bathroom, Nia goes in the bathroom with me and lies down on her back and waits for me to take my foot and rub it on her belly. And it's not just for me; everyone in my house knows that as soon as they get up to go to the bathroom that Nia will be lying on her back right beneath their feet waiting for her belly scratch.

—TOMIKO CHAPRON
MARINA DEL REY, CALIFORNIA
🐾 NIA, SHIH TZU, 3

MY DOG HAD A CHAIR that we bought especially for her, and she knew it. If anyone else sat in the chair, even if she wasn't using it, she would bark and bark at them until they finally got up and gave it back to her.

—BETH STURGEON
CHICAGO, MISSOURI
🐾 HEATHER

FAYTH, a Border Collie, is fond of herding sheep ... and tennis balls.

TERI THOMPSON (OWNER)
SIMI VALLEY, CALIFORNIA

IF YOU TELL BENVY "give me a hug," she jumps up and puts her paws on your belly so you can hug her. Everyone thinks it is so cute. She also can give high fives. You just put your hand up and say "Benvy, high five" and she jumps up and gives you a high five with her paw. That makes even our friends who don't really like dogs say "awwww."

—EMILY MASON
CINCINNATI, OHIO
🐕 BENVY, BLACK LABRADOR-CHOW CHOW MIX, 7

* * * * * * * * *

My dog's very good at falling asleep on the porch at a moment's notice, but I'm not sure that qualifies as a trick.

—TED VALKO
CHURCHILL, OHIO
🐕 9

* * * * * * * * *

MY DOGS, BUSTER AND KODA, sing on command. If there is a music box and you turn it on, they will sing to it. Or if you say, "Okay sing," then they will both start barking at each other, then sing.

—TERRI BRINK
SANTA CLARITA, CALIFORNIA
🐕 BUSTER, 4 🐕 KODA, 3, AUSTRALIAN SHEPHERDS

HUNTER TAUGHT HIMSELF to ride a skateboard; he rides around with the kids in the neighborhood. I actually had to buy him his own skateboard because the other kids didn't like him using theirs. He has all four paws on the board and he barks the entire time he's riding.

—SUSIE BROWN
FILLMORE, CALIFORNIA
🐕 HUNTER, 3 🐕 BODIE, 1, SHELTIES

MY GRANDDAUGHTER TAUGHT Cobber the funniest trick. Since Cobber loves to swim, she wanted him to dive into the pool at exactly the same time she did. She taught him to stand right next to the pool while she was on the diving board. Then she would count, "1...2...3," and they would both jump into the pool. Cobber does it every single time.

—LINDA KORBEL
CULVER CITY, CALIFORNIA
🐕 A.J., 12, 🐕 ADDIE, 12, GOLDEN RETRIEVERS
🐕 COBBER, LABRADOODLE, 16

OUR DOG CREATED A SPORT we call "ottoman surfing." When she comes inside full of energy, she runs through the kitchen and into the family room, then jumps on our ottoman and rides it as it slides all the way across the room on the hardwood floor.

—C.A.
CINCINNATI, OHIO
🐕 SYDNEY, SHEPHERD MIX, 8

Aleria can sing. If you start to howl she will howl along with you. Occasionally, if you just tell her to sing, she will do it.

—TIM POWELL
OAKDALE, MINNESOTA
🐕 ALERIA, MIXED BREED, 9

MY SHIH TZU, CHARLIE, was able to say, "Mama." I used to say, "I'm going to take her on David Letterman," but I know she wouldn't do it there.

—LOUISE BREW
VENICE, CALIFORNIA
🐕 BASIL, 3 🐕 MEMPHIS, 1
🐕 FANNIE, 14 🐕 CHARLIE, 13, SHIH TZUS

* * * * * * * *

One of Sam's crowd-pleasing tricks was to balance a ball on her nose. She won "Pet of the Game" at an Indianapolis Colts game when she balanced a football on her nose.

—AMY CHANDLER
COLUMBUS, INDIANA

* * * * * * * *

MELLOW IS A REALLY FUNNY DOG. He likes to stand on his two back legs as if he were human. And while he's standing on his back legs, he spins around. I swear, he looks like a little kid trying to get dizzy.

—MARSHA
LOS ANGELES, CALIFORNIA
🐕 MELLOW, PUG, 3

ALMOST PERFECT

When Sebastian was a puppy, I decided to train him to ring chimes whenever he had to go outside. I placed the chimes by the door, and every time we were about to go out, I would put a treat behind the chimes to teach him how to ring them using his nose. A few weeks went by and he hadn't used the chimes on his own. One afternoon, I heard the chimes and ran toward the door. You can imagine how proud I was. When I got there, Sebastian was sitting there so nicely and his tail was wagging; clearly, he was proud as well. It took only a second for me to realize that Sebastian had gotten the entire thing backward—he had peed in the house and then rung the chimes, as if to say, "Cleanup on aisle seven!"

—KATE
CHICAGO, ILLINOIS
SEBASTIAN, GREATER SWISS MOUNTAIN DOG, 3

MOOSE AND ME

I have an Australian Shepherd named Moose who has been deaf since birth. Most deaf dogs are put to sleep because they are thought to be aggressive, impossible to train, and unpredictable. I wouldn't hear of it. Three and a half years later, Moose understands sign language commands and is relatively well trained. I am not sure if it is in spite of her disability or perhaps because of it, but Moose is especially sensitive to the people around her.

Last summer, Moose started paying a lot more attention to me than usual. When I would be lying in bed, watching TV, she wouldn't stop licking my face ... and in the same place on my chin every time. I thought it was kind of odd, until I saw a TV show about dogs who are able to smell cancer. I was still skeptical, but I went to the dermatologist and asked to have that spot on my jaw biopsied. My doctor wasn't thrilled with the idea, noting that there was nothing visible on the surface to worry about. I insisted, and less than a week later, at the age of 27, was diagnosed with basal cell carcinoma. I was diagnosed soon after with two other cases of melanoma. I'm happy to report that I've had three surgeries and am doing well now. It may sound strange, but, I feel as if Moose paid me back for saving her life by saving mine.

—SARAH
VAN NUYS, CALIFORNIA
🐕 MOOSE, AUSTRALIAN SHEPHERD, 3

WHEN I WAS GROWING UP, my family had a dog named Jacques who had a penchant for my mom's homemade oatmeal raisin cookies. In fact, he liked them so much that he was willing to do tricks to get one. He was a hunting dog, so he was very smart and able to listen to commands. My dad taught him to balance a cookie on his nose until we gave him the cue, and then he'd flick it up in the air and catch it in his mouth.

—JENNIFER KUSHNIER
BETHLEHEM, PENNSYLVANIA
🐕 GRETA, PUG, 4
🐕 JACQUES, BRITTANY SPANIEL, 14

• • • • • • • •

MY YOUNGEST DOG is a Cocker Spaniel named Dolly. She was named after Barbra Streisand's role in *Hello, Dolly*. When you sing "Hello, Dolly" to her she goes crazy. I sing to her all the time.

—JANICE
SAN DIEGO, CALIFORNIA
🐕 TOKEN, 4 🐕 DOLLY, 1, COCKER SPANIELS
🐕 EMME, 🐕 BUSTER 🐕 VITA, ROTTWEILERS

• • • • • • • •

OUR DOG'S FUNNIEST TRICK was resting with her front legs flat on the ground and her hind end straight up in the air. She smiled and thought she was cute.

—PAT
ROSEVILLE, MINNESOTA
🐕 JILL, GERMAN SHEPHERD, 5
🐕 PUPPY, 3 🐕 MAGGIE, 11, MIXED BREEDS

Two of our dogs, Simba and Cocoa, play tug-of-war with a rope. They pull each other all over the yard.

—DEBBIE RINGGOLD,
GEORGIA
🐕 PRISSY,
AMERICAN
ESKIMO, 1
🐕 GOLD, 12
🐕 SIMBA, 1,
YELLOW LABS
🐕 COCOA,
CHOCOLATE LAB, 1

MY DOG HAS GOTTEN pretty proficient at catching a Frisbee. It wasn't nearly as hard as I thought it would be to teach him. The whole secret is just in repetition. I guess it's true what they say about practice making perfect. We are lucky because we live right across the road from a big, flat open field where I can fling the Frisbee all day long. The dog at first just sat there looking at me when I threw it. But then I started to chase it after I threw it and the dog would follow. He eventually started catching them once in a while, and now he catches almost all of them.

—ANONYMOUS
FLORENCE, KENTUCKY
🐕 POODLE, 4

Since Cocoe can't talk, we taught him to use sneezes. He lets us know he has to go out by sneezing. Whenever he needs anything, he sneezes.

—BARRY TURCHEN
LOS ANGELES, CALIFORNIA
🐕 COCOE, MIXED BREED, 14

SPEAK! NO, SING!

My dog Aquarius had an incredible singing talent. I had called in sick from work to take him to a Purina Dog Chow contest in which the dog with the best singing voice would be featured on a bag of dog food. With great confidence, I entered the staging area, knowing how well he could sing, speak, roll over—do anything—right on cue. But when I saw the TV cameras there for the event, I feared my boss might see me on TV, so I had my husband go up on the stage with Aquarius, even though he was really my dog, and Ed didn't understand him all that well. Well, the big moment came, and my husband clearly commanded Aquarius to speak! Obediently, my proud pooch did speak, but of course, it didn't count as a song and, unfortunately, there were no second chances. His career was over before it began. And I lost my chance to be a Hollywood stage mother.

—CONNIE THROOP
ST. LOUIS, MISSOURI
🐕 AQUARIUS, LAB MIX
🐕 PRINCESSA, MIXED BREED

ESP DOG

BARKLEY IS VERY SENSITIVE TO PEOPLE'S NEEDS. One time
my son, who just turned 13, was very sick with bronchitis
and Barkley just parked himself at my son's side as if
protecting him from what was invading his space.

—LAURA
LOS ANGELES, CALIFORNIA
🐕 BARKLEY, MINIATURE LABRADOODLE, 2

* * * * * * * *

I DON'T KNOW IF IT IS A SIXTH SENSE OR WHAT, but our
dog sure can tell when a storm is about to hit. And she
always knows long before I do. She scrambles into some
corner and pants, and that's when we know there's going
to be some rough weather, even if it might not look like
it outside.

—TIM POWELL
OAKDALE, MINNESOTA
🐕 ALERIA, MIXED BREED, 9

* * * * * * * *

MELLOW CAN FEEL ME on a whole other level than touch.
He often keeps to himself, but whenever I'm upset, especially when I'm crying, he comes over and licks my face.
I swear, Mellow would curl up next to me and lick every
single tear until my face was dry.

—MARSHA
LOS ANGELES, CALIFORNIA
🐕 MELLOW, PUG, 3

I LIVED IN MANHATTAN in a fourth-floor walk-up with my wife and my dog, Frankie. I traveled a lot for work, and sometimes I would be gone for weeks at a time. But when I was on my way home, Frankie knew it. I would be in a cab, a few blocks from my home and Frankie would just go nuts. My wife thought it was uncanny. She said that every single time I started on my way home, Frankie knew it.

—JOHN
LOS ANGELES, CALIFORNIA
FRANK, WESTIE, 14
LUCY, AUSTRALIAN CATTLE DOG, 12

ONE NIGHT MY WIFE AND I WERE FIGHTING. I was sitting on our bed and my wife was sitting on a chair in the bedroom. Cindy knew we were at odds, so she decided that she needed to mediate. She came over to me and tapped me with her paw. Then she went over to my wife and tapped her with her paw. She repeated this over and over again until my wife finally got into bed with me.

—MALCOLM
LOS ANGELES, CALIFORNIA
CINDY, 7   TRACY, 10, BOXERS

ONE NIGHT I WAS TALKING TO MY HUSBAND and told him I was thinking of taking Mitzi to work with me the next day. That was pretty much the entire conversation. The next morning when I got ready to leave, Mitzi ran out the gate and over to my car. She had never done that before; she normally stays on the porch and watches me leave.

—CONNIE LARRICK
RHOME, TEXAS
🐕 DOC, 12 🐕 JERRY JOE, 14, COCKER SPANIELS
🐕 OSCAR, 12 🐕 RIPPY BEAR, 7, DACHSHUNDS
🐕 MITZI, DACHSHUND-CHIHUAHUA MIX, 7
🐕 BUDDY, TIBETAN TERRIER MIX, 6

• • • • • • • • •

BECAUSE OF MY JOB, I spend weeks and even months at a time away from home. Greta, always knows when I'm leaving for a long time, even when I don't have a suitcase or a packed bag. I know that she knows because when I look for her to say goodbye, she's hiding under the couch or in her crate where she feels safe. She acts the same way when my husband leaves for a few days, but she never hides when one of us is just going to the store or making another small trip.

—JENNIFER KUSHNIER
BETHLEHEM, PENNSYLVANIA
🐕 GRETA, PUG, 4
🐕 JACQUES, BRITTANY SPANIEL, 14

SAM WOULD LIE DOWN about 10 feet from me and stare, anxiously awaiting the ball. I would roll it to him and when it was about a foot away, he would stand up and pounce on it, put it in his mouth, and start trying to chew it. I would let him chew for a minute, then say, "Sam, throw me the ball!" He would put it down between his front paws, lift one paw and move it in front of him, then lunge at it with both front paws, pushing it—sometimes bouncing it—to me. Then he would lie down and start the process over. I am sure Sam simply "threw" me the ball when he was ready, but I had people convinced he did it on command!

—BILL WHELAN
FREEPORT, MAINE
🐕 MAGGIE, COLLIE MIX, 14
🐕 BUTTONE, DALMATIAN, 4
🐕 SAM, LHASA APSO-POODLE MIX, 14

MY DOG, POPPY, can make a whole chicken disappear! One night, I made a four-pound rotisserie chicken and left it on the counter. When I came back, the whole thing was gone—bones, twine, everything! Just a spot of grease was all that remained on the foil that he had spread out on the kitchen floor.

—NIKKI GLENN
ST. LOUIS, MISSOURI
🐕 POPPY, MIXED BREED, 4

SINCE WE FIRST BROUGHT HER HOME, Hailey has gone to work with my husband Jason. At first he carried her in a small duffel bag. Hailey became accustomed to going to work in this bag. Every time Jason got this duffel bag out, she knew that it was time to go to work with Jason. We threw out the duffel bag because the zipper had broken, and hadn't used a duffel bag with Hailey for quite some time. But just the other day, I bought a new one, for myself. I brought it home, and she climbed right into the bag, even before I took the tags off and removed the packaging. She stared at me, with a look that said, "Okay, I'm ready to go now!" I put her blanket and some toys in with her, and she slept in there the rest of the night, just to make sure we didn't leave home without her!

—HEATHER NELSON
PLYMOUTH, MINNESOTA
🐕 HAILEY, MIXED BREED, 1

Hero Dog

N o matter how often we hear stories of the courageous, amazing, intuitive, and life-saving exploits of dogs—especially those of our average, normal, companions—we are astounded all over again. These dogs, with their senses apparently tuned exclusively to our personal channels, are watching out for us. So, the next time you glare impatiently at your sacked-out, lazy pup, remember: he's probably monitoring the local weather conditions in case of an impending tornado. Give him a biscuit!

AT ABOUT 2 A.M., Mickey woke us up during a storm. He doesn't like bad weather anyway, but this time he was really acting wild; pacing, crying, and jumping onto the bed and back down again. One of my sons offered to take him outside, and when he opened the door, he realized our house was on fire! My husband, both our sons, and I managed to get out and run to a safe distance from the house. A few minutes later, our garage exploded. Very quickly, the fire completely consumed the entire house and it burned to the ground. I don't know what would have happened had Mickey not sensed the danger and gotten us out of the house. He saved our lives.

—ALLYN HEFFNER
CHESTERFIELD, MISSOURI
🐕 MICKEY, 12

• • • • • • • •

AT SEVEN YEARS OLD, Kaycee became a therapy dog. She visits cancer patients at UCI Medical Center. I knew that therapy work would be good for her because she loves people. We were visiting a patient who was going to chemotherapy for the first time and did not want to go at all, but Kaycee came to visit and encouraged her to follow through.

—ROBIN WINDLINGER
FULLERTON, CALIFORNIA
🐕 KAYCEE, BERNESE MOUNTAIN DOG, 9

WHEN I WAS GROWING UP in Connecticut, my family had a dog named Binx. In fourth grade I had a big falling-out with my parents, and to get back at them I decided to run away. I packed up my sleeping bag and headed off with a box of chocolate granola bars and a six-pack of juice. Binx was on the outskirts of the property as I left. I said goodbye to her and walked maybe one street over and into the woods, where I proceeded to set up camp. I was out there for more than a day; meanwhile, my parents were freaking out and had called the cops to look for me. I was scared myself, especially sleeping alone in the woods at night. Early the next morning, I heard the noise of something coming through the woods, and suddenly my dog was there. Our property had an electric fence, but she'd run through it to find me. This was like a wake-up call; I realized I needed to go home immediately. I packed up camp and went back to my house, where my parents were happy to see me.

—CRIS
NEW YORK, NEW YORK
🐕 BINX, SOFT COATED WHEATEN TERRIER, 13

* * * * * * * * *

I'D JUST COME OUT OF THE HOSPITAL for back surgery and Hannah decided she was going to be my nurse. When I lay down on the bed she would lie beside me; when I rolled over and moaned because I was in pain, she would kiss me all over and check me out to make sure I was okay.

—SUSAN KERNS
SAN DIEGO, CALIFORNIA
🐕 HANNAH, 6

WE LIVE BY A NURSING HOME, and when it's nice outside a lot of the patients sit on the sidewalk in their wheelchairs. One day, Barkly and I were on a walk and he decided to say hello to a woman sitting there. He approached her and her face lit up so much. She was so out of it, I don't think she even saw me. But when Barkly put his paws on her lap, she bent her head over to kiss him and said over and over, "I love you, I love you." Since then, Barkly and I make it a habit to walk by and say hello. I think the people there look forward to our visits.

—KRISTI
LOS ANGELES, CALIFORNIA
🐕 BARKLY, JACK RUSSELL, 4

* * * * * * * *

Hunter does therapy work at a convalescent home. There is a man there who doesn't have any legs. Hunter climbs up onto the man's lap and I push the two of them around in the wheelchair.

—SUSIE BROWN
FILLMORE, CALIFORNIA
🐕 HUNTER, 3 🐕 BODIE, 1, SHELTIES

I AM A THERAPIST and Maggie sits in with me on every session. It's amazing how she helps calm so many people. If someone is upset, she notices; when they notice that she notices, they apologize and I have to say its OK. My patients love to pet her because it's really calming for them.

—JOAN BALLON
LOS ANGELES, CALIFORNIA
🐾 MAGGIE, 14 🐾 SAM, 13, BRITTANY SPANIELS
🐾 SPEX, AUSTRALIAN SHEPHERD, 2

• • • • • • • •

LUCKY'S A VERY CALM DOG. The only time I've seen him get excited is when he wants more food: He does this little tap dance, hopping quickly from foot to foot. We joke that he escaped from the circus. One day, I was in my basement apartment on the phone. He was out in the yard and I could see him going from window to window, looking in. He was extremely fussy, which is completely out of character. This must have gone on for at least 10 minutes. I thought he would stop, but he didn't give up. He kept stepping toward me, leading with his head, looking toward the yard, then looking at me and then looking back to the yard. Then he ran toward the fence. I started following him, and that's when I saw that my cat was hanging upside down, crying weakly, his left leg sandwiched in the fence slot! I don't know what would have happened if Lucky hadn't alerted me. After that, I started calling him Lassie.

—KATHY GERMANA
FARMINGVILLE, NEW YORK
🐾 LUCKY, MIXED BREED, 7

Cobber once saved our son's dog from drowning in our pool. Cobber loves to swim, but our son's dog never could learn how.

—LINDA KORBEL
CULVER CITY,
CALIFORNIA
🐾 A.J., 12
🐾 ADDIE,
12, GOLDEN
RETRIEVERS
🐾 COBBER,
LABRADOODLE,
16

BEWARE OF DOG— OWNER, TOO!

On Broadway in downtown Manhattan, Tristan and I were walking on the sidewalk early one Sunday morning. They had shut down the street for a bike race, but this guy was riding his bike on the sidewalk, which was illegal and really stupid. The guy saw me, but he didn't see Tristan. He had to stop suddenly and he fell off his bike. His head went between two utility poles. I was really scared; I thought he broke his neck. Well, he was OK, and came up screaming at *me*! I told him he was a total jerk for riding on the sidewalk when the whole street was closed down for the bikers. I kept walking, but he began to follow me. I turned and confronted him and asked why he was following me. He didn't answer, but kept getting closer. So I said, "How would you like an 80-pound pit bull up your ass?" This stopped him cold in his tracks—Tristan sat next to me and began to do a low growl and show the guy his teeth. No more problems after that—Tristan rescued me from a potential attacker!

—JULIA
NEW YORK, NEW YORK
🐕 TRISTAN, MIXED BREED, 1

BUSTER HAS REALLY GOOD EARS. One night, my cat was in distress out front. I didn't know it, but Buster knew, and went totally crazy. He ran to the front door and when I didn't follow he came back to try and get me again. I couldn't figure out what he was doing, so I opened the door and saw my cat on her back, and there was another cat, or maybe a raccoon, attacking her. As soon as the animal saw me it ran off. I brought the cat inside and Buster snuggled with it and loved it; the cat was OK.

—TERRI BRINK
SANTA CLARITA, CALIFORNIA
🐕 BUSTER, 4 🐕 KODA, 3, AUSTRALIAN SHEPHERDS

ONE WEEKEND, MY FATHER, my brother, and a friend of theirs decided to go hunting and went up to a cabin in the woods, taking our dog, Sultan. They had never been hunting and knew nothing about it. When they arrived at the cabin, they decided they wanted to camp out. So they gathered up their gear and loaded themselves with canned food. They set up camp someplace very far into the woods. When it was time to eat, they realized that all they had was canned food, but no can opener. Then they realized that they had no idea where they were or how to get back to the cabin. So the three helpless men turned to Sultan and asked for help. Sultan immediately got up and led them back to the cabin.

—NORMA
LOS ANGELES, CALIFORNIA
🐕 LOGAN, PUG, 7
🐕 SULTAN, BOXER, 10

HAILEY, a mixed-breed dog from Minnesota, ready for anything.

HEATHER NELSON (OWNER)
PLYMOUTH, MINNESOTA

I RUN A SMALL FARM IN SOUTHERN NEW MEXICO. Tocaya has been with me since day one. I'm a naturopathic physician and a homeopath, and I realized a puppy was an incredible healer. She came to the office with me every day and would hang out. There would be times she would be out in the front office and other times she'd want to come back into the consulting room and be with us. If people were emotionally upset, worried or anxious, that's usually when she would come in. She had a way of taking that energy into herself. In fact, her nickname is Dr. Dog.

—JOANIE
EMBUDO, NEW MEXICO
🐕 TOCAYA, AKITA-GERMAN SHEPHERD MIX, 9

• • • • • • • •

YEARS AGO, my husband and I had just gotten back from a car trip with our two dogs, Willy and Yvan. I went into the house with the dogs, while my husband was transferring from the car into his wheelchair. Willy became extremely agitated and was barking his head off. I kept telling him to be quiet and then I tried to ignore him. Fifteen minutes later, he was still barking. I went to the door to check on what my husband was doing that was taking so long, and I saw that he had missed his wheelchair and had fallen to the ground; that's what Willy was trying to tell me.

—EILEEN GRASING
SAN DIEGO, CALIFORNIA
🐕 WILLIE, 8 🐕 YVAN, 11

CANINE COPS & FIREFIGHTERS

WE WERE SOUND ASLEEP. It was between two and three in the morning, and Duncan started pestering me. He usually sleeps in bed with us, but he got up and was sticking his snout under my arm to make me get up. So I got up and told my husband I was taking the dog outside. But when we got outside, it was clear he didn't have to do anything. He was just staring at the house next door, which had been empty for a while. I looked up and in my foggy mind, I thought, "Hey, look at all the steam coming out from under that roof." Then I noticed the flames shooting up through the second-floor windows, illuminating everything. I ran back in the house, called 911, and the firefighters came out and put the fire out. I really think it saved our house and the other houses nearby, because we're quite close together. A few days later, one of the neighbors sent Duncan a bunch of pretty yellow tulips with a card that said, "Thanks for saving the neighborhood." And just last week a fireman at the nearby station saw me walking Duncan and said, "Is that the dog that detected the fire?"

—DEBORAH GIRARD
MINNEAPOLIS, MINNESOTA
🐕 DUNCAN, ENGLISH SETTER, 1

ONE NIGHT IN OUR APARTMENT, our dog was going crazy; barking, running up and down the stairs, and coming in to try to wake me. I had been sound asleep, but I got up to see why she was barking. I looked out the window and saw the shadow of a person. I called the police, who came, looked around, and left. But Hannah was still going crazy. Then I noticed that the window was open behind the curtains. I called the police again, and we went outside, and found the contents of my purse scattered all over. Someone had opened the window, reached in with a garden rake, and lifted out my purse, along with a wedding present that had been sitting on the table. Hannah had scared this guy away, but the sad part is that he went on that night to break into another woman's apartment. He attacked her and stole her car. The police caught him in her car, with my purse. When they caught him, he started cursing out "that big black dog" for alerting everyone. I've always thought that if it hadn't been for Hannah, I would have been that other woman.

—STACEY
MINNEAPOLIS, MINNESOTA
🐕 HANNAH, LABRADOR-GERMAN SHEPHERD MIX

BOGEY IS A THERAPY DOG. He goes to the rehab center a lot. I dress him up on holidays before he goes on his visits. One Halloween, I dressed him up as a devil. He had a red cape that looked really cool because he's coal black. It also had pointy ears that he wore. He has bunny ears for Easter and reindeer antlers for Christmas.

—CHERYL BALL
CAPE GIRARDEAU, MISSOURI
BOGEY, LABRADOR, 5

Pretty/ Handsome Dog

All puppies are cute; we know this. And every owner thinks his own dog is adorable. But really, how many dogs are so good-looking that they literally stop traffic? Amazing though it is, several of them are described in this chapter. Those eyes! Those ears! That tail! We know it's only fur-deep, but we're grateful for great-looking dogs.

WHEN I PICK OUT CLOTHES FOR WALRUS, she runs towards the clothes because she knows she looks good in them. She also knows she gets more attention when she wears them. She has a lot of funny outfits, like a little bumblebee outfit with a black tutu.

> —AMY HUANG
> SANTA MONICA, CALIFORNIA
> 🐕 WALRUS, YORKIE, 2

• • • • • • • • •

I ONCE WENT TO AN EVENT where they had a pet psychic. The psychic relayed to me some of the questions that Ketzi needed to have answered, and one important one was, "Am I really as pretty as my mom keeps telling me that I am?" I know I'm biased, but she is the prettiest dog I've ever seen.

> —MARLA
> LOS ANGELES, CALIFORNIA
> 🐕 KETZI, POODLE-MALTESE MIX, 6

• • • • • • • •

MUSHU PLAYS HIS CUTENESS CARD all the time. He cocks his head to the side and gives a little whiny talk to get people's attention. Tag is the biggest beggar I've ever seen. If I take him to a party, he works the entire crowd for treats. He has that brown-eyed look that makes you want to give all of your food to him. He's a total professional.

> —GENEVIEVE YATES
> CAPE TOWN, SOUTH AFRICA
> 🐕 TAG, COCKER SPANIEL, 10
> 🐕 MUSHU, SHIH TZU, 3

SEBASTIAN GETS A LOT OF ATTENTION when we walk down the street, mainly because he weighs 140 pounds. We were walking one evening and passed a group of 14-year-old girls. The group started commenting, "Look at that dog, he is so cute, what a handsome boy ... " Sebastian was looking at the group, tail wagging, and enjoying the attention. As we passed them, he continued to stare and forgot to look where he was going. He was extremely embarrassed when he walked directly into a garbage can.

—KATE
CHICAGO, ILLINOIS
🐕 SEBASTIAN, GREATER SWISS MOUNTAIN DOG, 3

• • • • • • • •

MONTY IS A MIXED BREED with a gray-and-black wirehair coat, but the top of his head is soft and downy. He also has a "lazy" ear, so one folds forward and one folds back. When we are out on family walks with our one-year-old son, inevitably someone will stop us and say, "Isn't he so cute!" Just when we're about to reply that we think our son is cute, too, the person will ask what breed he is. I try to laugh it off, but I can't help but think, "Is my dog better looking than my baby?"

—BETH BROWN
CINCINNATI, OHIO
🐕 MONTY, TERRIER-POODLE MIX, 5

Our dog Lady was well aware of how everything matched on her: She had a brown coat, brown eyes, brown nose and brown nails.

—LISA
MCKEARNEY
LOS ANGELES,
CALIFORNIA
🐕 LADY,
MIXED BREED,
16

SPRINGERS TYPICALLY HAVE VERY LONG HAIR, especially on the backs of their legs and tails. I always get comments on how beautiful she is with her long hair. Then I had her hair cut short and people now comment on how beautiful her color is.

—TRACY LEE ALLEN
FREDERICK, MARYLAND
SPIRIT, ENGLISH SPRINGER SPANIEL, 2

- - - - - - - -

I groom Miles myself. We play barber-shop, and while I'm grooming him I tell him how handsome he is and he admires himself in the mirror.

—PAULA
INGLEWOOD, CALIFORNIA
MILES, MALTEPOO, 2

- - - - - - - -

JAX IS SUCH A GOOD LOOKING DOG that it's really irritating; it takes me about five times longer to get anywhere I need to go since people constantly want to take pictures of him. When I was living in New York, I actually had people stop in the middle of a busy Manhattan intersection and want to take pictures with him.

—JESSICA
LOS ANGELES, CALIFORNIA
JAX, LABRADOODLE, 1

MELLOW KNOWS HOW HANDSOME HE IS. I know this because of the way he walks or prances. He holds his head really high and walks around like a little pony. For the first week after he is groomed he tries really hard not to get himself dirty. If there's mud on our walk he tries to go around it, and does the same thing for puddles. He knows how good he looks and wants to stay that way for as long as possible.

—MARSHA
LOS ANGELES, CALIFORNIA
🐕 MELLOW, PUG, 3

* * * * * * * *

WHEN RUBY'S MOM HAD HER LITTER, the breeder determined that Ruby didn't have the characteristics to carry on the lineage. But it makes no difference to her; in her mind, she's a high-class show dog. Ruby's grandfather won at Westminster, and evidence of that gene is tangible. She always carries herself as if the judges are passing by. She has a haughtiness and a prancing walk that says, "Don't you just adore me?" She wants to be admired and fawned over, but she doesn't want to be touched—especially after she's been groomed. It's like, "Please, don't mess up the hair!"

—BONNIE SOLLOG
FLORAL PARK, NEW YORK
🐕 RUBY, STANDARD POODLE

SOPHIE, a Lab mix living in Atlanta, Georgia, is so beautiful she stops traffic. It's easy to see why.

IT WAS EASY TO HELP STANLEY maintain his good looks. When I took him to the vet for a bath and haircut, I would place him on the counter and the attendant would secure him with his leash or a tether. But when the doctor walked in, she would always remove the tether and inform the attendant, "You don't need this with Stanley." Stanley would stand there motionless while they trimmed and bathed him, and they always threw in a complete physical for free.

—RAY
FLORISSANT, MISSOURI
🐕 STANLEY, COCKER SPANIEL-GOLDEN RETRIEVER MIX, 13

• • • • • • • •

SOPHIE IS SO BEAUTIFUL she stops traffic. Literally. She's a Lab mix, and her fur is a chocolate-brown color, but she has these long wisps of lighter brown hair on her ears, tail and at the back of her legs. Her toes are white. She also has very pink lips. She is all girl. People always mention how pretty she is, but I remember one time we were crossing a busy street with her and this older man crossing in the opposite direction had to stop—despite the oncoming traffic—and admire her. He said, "That's one pretty dog."

—J.A.
ATLANTA, GEORGIA
🐕 SOPHIE, LABRADOR-AUSTRALIAN SHEPHERD MIX, 2
🐕 CLIFTON, MIXED BREED, 10

Nia knows she's hot. When my mom has her groomed, Nia acts different: She knows when she's clean and smelling good.

—TOMIKO
CHAPRON
MARINA DEL
REY,
CALIFORNIA
🐕 NIA, SHIH
TZU, 3

HUNTER'S EYES ARE BIGGER than her head and her ears touch the ground, making her off-the-chart cute! Our teenage boys used to take Hunter with them to as many places as they could, because she was known as the "chick magnet." Everywhere they took Hunter, all the girls would want to pet her and hold her and ask about her. She was a great icebreaker for them.

—SUSAN RICCIARDI
CINCINNATI, OHIO
🐕 HUNTER, BEAGLE, 8

* * * * * * * *

LOGAN KNOWS THAT SHE IS A KNOCKOUT. My husband and I travel with her and when we are walking through the airport she struts her stuff like she's the Queen of Sheba. When she's on the plane, she sits on my lap and the flight attendants make a fuss over her.

—NORMA
LOS ANGELES, CALIFORNIA
🐕 LOGAN, PUG, 7
🐕 SULTAN, BOXER, 10

* * * * * * * *

CASEY'S PRETTY ADORABLE by any standards, but what makes her really stand out is her walk. She doesn't walk; she prances. One day a stranger stopped me and said, "Did you know your dog walks like an Arabian horse?"

—SHAROLYN WIEBE
VANCOUVER, CANADA
🐕 CASEY, SHELTIE, 9

Triumph-Over-Adversity Dog

Not every dog is a lucky dog. Some just can't seem to get a break—that is, until they meet up with the right human. This chapter portrays some great dogs with great big problems, but the people who love them help them through. Nothing but happy endings to these stories.

MATY SHOULD NOT BE HERE. She should have died at three weeks of age in the motel room where she was abandoned. She should have caught the deadly Parvo virus at six weeks. When a misdiagnosed Staphylococcus infection destroyed the tendons and ligaments in her left hind leg, she was supposed to pass away—but she didn't. A financially strapped Humane Society of Central Oregon could have euthanized Maty at 7 weeks. Instead, the shelter paid for the amputation that gave Maty her first step toward becoming a local celebrity.

At Maty's first residence, she learned to drag herself around on the floor. Her second family included two 10-year-old Australian shepherds who could run like the wind. At seven months, Maty was up for the challenge; soon she could outrun her companions.

Today, Maty is perhaps the best-known dog in Bend, Oregon. To observers at the Disc Dog Championships in Atlanta, however, Maty and her human companion were just another rookie team that would at best catch a few short throws and get some sympathy applause.

Instead, catching everything her friend could throw, Maty finished seventh out of 24 in her first world championship event. She has promised her fans that she'll be back . . . even if she's really not supposed to be there.

—LYNNE OUCHIDA
BEND, OREGON
🐕 MATY, 6, MIXED BREED

ONE LUCKY DOG

Sometimes I think my dog Maggie is a cat, because she's had so many lives. Two years ago she had a tumor. The vet said that if it had been any other dog, he would have looked at the tumor, sewed her back up and put her down. He knew, though, that Maggie's spirit would pull her through. He spent five hours in surgery with her, cutting out a tumor in her spine and hip. Then, a few months ago, Maggie contracted a terrible case of pneumonia. She was 14 years old, and I really thought that this was it; I'd be taking her to the hospital to put her down. She was in the hospital for a week, hooked up to an I.V. At the end of her treatment she developed vestibular disease, which hits older dogs acutely. When this happened I was certain once again that our next trip to the vet would be her last. But the doctor put her on some medicine and she's fine now. She's 14 and a half years old, and I know she's going to make it to 15.

—JOAN BALLON
LOS ANGELES, CALIFORNIA
🐕 MAGGIE, 14 🐕 SAM, 13, BRITTANY SPANIELS
🐕 SPEX, AUSTRALIAN SHEPHERD, 2

A COUPLE OF WEEKS INTO DOG OWNERSHIP (already a challenge for my never-had-a-pet husband) I sacrificed my marriage and sanity by bringing my dog from Minnesota to California for our planned family reunion. I stuffed her into a carrying case that she hated and the vet-approved tranquilizers weren't kicking in. After a rough stretch we had barely made it through check-in and security when the dog carrier's zipper broke. After boarding the plane there were whines and yelps. My husband said, "This is not working," and I was unsure if he meant Lucy or us. Our luck changed in the back row of the plane, when the flight attendant told us to take her out of her case and keep her in the middle seat. The couple across the way gave us beef jerky, ice cubes to cool her off, and lots of encouragement. Finally, our little puppy calmed down and looked at us with a new expression—trust—and fell asleep. We were so proud of the little fur ball we just couldn't stop petting her. We even held hands again, figuring that since we made it through this we'd pretty much be married forever. A few hours later we introduced our parents to their grand-dog.

—JENNIFER KRAMER
MINNEAPOLIS, MINNESOTA
🐕 LUCILLE BELLE, 1

MATY, the three-legged wonder dog, competes paw-to-paw with other canine disc-catching athletes.

LYNNE OUCHIDA (OWNER)
BEND, OREGON

PUP GOING UP!

A LONG LEASH SAVED MY DOG. We were staying at a hotel that allowed animals, and I got into the elevator with the dog on its leash. As the door started to close, the dog backed out. The retractable leash was going up with the elevator and this little, 20-pound Westie was being dragged up and strangled. I hit the emergency button to stop the elevator, and ran up to the next floor. There were two workers helping us. We measured the distance between floors, which was 26 feet, and that was exactly the length of the leash.

—MARIA
SOUTH BRUNSWICK, NEW JERSEY
MAGGIE, 8 GUS, 2

• • • • • • • • •

RECENTLY, MY THREE KIDS went to walk our dog, Maxi. They let the leash drag, and the elevator door in our building closed, with the leash getting stuck. So, Maxi was slowly being pulled up with the elevator, and my kids were freaking out and screaming. He had on a body leash, so he wasn't choking. My 11-year-old daughter was pulling on the leash, so it broke, snapped back and cut her finger. She needed 13 stitches, but she saved our dog.

—DIANA
THE BRONX, NEW YORK
MAXIMILLION, MIXED BREED, 10

WHEN MY SON WAS IN FIFTH GRADE, he came home from school and announced that he wanted to get a dog. He and his father went to the pound and came back with the scrawniest, ugliest dog I had ever seen, a two-year-old, 11-pound, terrier mix. Because he was malnourished, his hair was coming out in patches. Cory named him Randall Cunningham after the football player and, although Randy could be a little nasty by growling and showing his teeth, we grew to love him. With our love and care he grew to be 22 pounds and loved to sing when Cory made a whistling sound by blowing on a blade of grass.

—CHAR LAVALETTE
RALEIGH, NORTH CAROLINA
🐕 GRIFFEY, BEAGLE, 8
🐕 RANDY, TERRIER MIX, 9

• • • • • • • • •

MY HOUSE WAS BURGLARIZED when Pinch was home alone. When I walked in, he had these orange markings all over his body and was panicking. I thought he had gotten into something. Then I went into the office and realized that we had been robbed and he had been pepper-sprayed. Before even calling to report the burglary to the cops I brought Pinch to the vet. When the handlers gave Pinch a bath, as soon as the water hit the pepper spray the fumes were all over everything. Pinch's eyes were affected a little bit; we had to put drops in his eyes for about a week. He was very skittish after this, but with lots of work he recovered.

—PINK
LOS ANGELES, CALIFORNIA
🐕 PINCH, 5 🐕 TAFFY
🐕 GRACIE, MIXED BREED, 1

INCREDIBLE JOURNEYS

"YOU'VE GOT TO STOP," I said to my husband as we drove out of the subdivision of our second home in Cabo San Lucas, Mexico, all dressed up for dinner. What looked at first like a cat was a small dog making its way across the road. This poor dog, a bundle of matted fur, protruding bones and sweet eyes, put her little paws around my neck and hugged me so tightly. We took her back to the house, gave her several baths and tried to find her owner. Two days later, we'd had no luck and we'd fallen so in love with her that we decided to take her home to St. Louis. Princessa was so little, we were able to put her into a cat-sized carrier and she stayed beneath our seats for the entire 2,000-mile trip.

—CONNIE THROOP
ST. LOUIS, MISSOURI
🐾 AQUARIUS, LAB MIX
🐾 PRINCESSA, MIXED BREED

• • • • • • • •

OUR DOG USED TO RUN AWAY A LOT. He would always squirm out of his collar with his nametag on it and leave it behind. The police in our town started to call him Houdini. Once, they found him in Newark, 12 miles away.

—BRITTANI BARTOK
UNION, NEW JERSEY
🐾 PUPALUP, 17
🐾 CUJO, MIXED BREED, 1

WE CAN TRUST OUR YELLOW LABRADOR, LULU, to stay in the yard, even when no one is watching. That is, until one day when I left the house to go for a walk with my daughter. I was about 10 blocks away when a woman in a minivan pulled up next to me as I pushed the stroller and said, "Do you have a yellow Lab?" I looked into her van to see Lulu hurling herself against the back windows. It turns out that Lulu tried to follow us but got lost and headed the wrong way. It was the only time she has ever wandered off, and it was to chase us, not to get away!

—MARISKA VAN AALST
EMMAUS, PENNSYLVANIA
🐕 LULU, LABRADOR, 7

• • • • • • • • •

MY WIFE, CYNDI, was about to have her first obstetrical appointment for our first daughter and I was going along. I had let Aleria out to do her business but forgot to chain her up. I was distracted by something for a moment, then realized she was nowhere to be found. We searched all over for her. After quite a while, we finally found her; she had been swimming in a pond and having a great time. But the worst part was how it made me feel: I'm going to become a dad and I can't even keep track of a dog!

—TIM POWELL
OAKDALE, MINNESOTA
🐕 ALERIA, MIXED BREED, 9

MY FRIEND AND I WOULD LET RACHEL ride in the back of a pickup truck because it has a cap on it, which means she's safe back there—or so we thought. She was riding in the back of the truck one day as we were driving over the Chesapeake Bay Bridge on our way home from a weekend at the beach. I turned around to give her a bone and she wasn't there. We drove to the tollbooth and told the collector that our dog had somehow managed to open the lock on the back and get out. We had to drive back over the bridge to the police barracks, and I spent the entire 20-mile drive hanging out the window in tears as I yelled Rachel's name. We reported her missing to the police, and by the time we made it back over the bridge, the toll collector told us the police had called and they had our dog. So we made the trip back over the bridge again and found Rachel safe and sound in a police car. She was found walking back over the bridge after falling out of the truck. Another driver saw her and called the police. She must have had an angel on her shoulder that day.

—MAUREEN HILL-HAUCH
FREDERICKSBURG, VIRGINIA
🐕 RACHEL, GERMAN SHEPHERD, 10

TEASE WAS ATTACKED by some other dogs in an obedience ring and sustained injuries we never thought he would overcome. He was doing the part of the competition where all of the dogs are lined up next to each other and have to lie down for a specified amount of time. During this exercise, the dog next to Tease decided to get up and come over. This prompted some of the other dogs to join, and eventually a fight broke out. There were seven dogs involved; my little guy was on the bottom. Tease injured his sciatica and was not able to walk correctly. We were determined to get better, and with lots of love and lots of therapy, seven months later we were back. Right now, we are actually running in an agility competition!

—TRACY KERNS
SAN DIEGO, CALIFORNIA
TEASE, FLAT COATED RETRIEVER, 7

BEAR WAS SHOT by a policeman outside our neighborhood convenience store. The bullet sped through Bear's left ear and into his rear paw. The shooting sparked an internal police investigation, a fine, and $5,000 in veterinary bills. Since then, Bear has suffered glaucoma, cancer, bladder stones, and vestibular disease, But it doesn't matter; having my best buddy by my side makes it all worthwhile.

—ANNA KILINSKI
ATLANTA, GEORGIA
BEAR, 8, LABRADOR RETRIEVER

SICK AS A DOG

MY DOG HAD ULCERS. I really never understood it. She lay in the sun all day and occasionally played tug-of-war with a stuffed pair of dice. That's not such a hard life, is it?

—ANDREA
TORONTO, CANADA
🐾 GREAT DANE

• • • • • • • •

OUR DOG HAS SEIZURES; he's on eight pills a day. When a seizure is coming on, he knows it, and puts his head on someone's leg. He just wants to be held until it's over.

—ANONYMOUS
NEW CITY, NEW YORK
🐾 BOOMER, GOLDEN RETRIEVER, 9

• • • • • • • •

COLUMBO HAD A TUMOR in his parathyroid gland. I knew something was wrong because his eating habits changed and he kept waking me up in the middle of the night to go to the bathroom. If he hadn't had surgery he would have had a host of other problems that would have led to organ failure. I just couldn't let that happen. I spent over $15,000 on his surgery and it was worth every penny.

—LISA ANSELL
BEVERLY HILLS, CALIFORNIA
🐾 COLUMBO, BASSET HOUND, 10

DUKE HAS TERRIBLE ALLERGIES. To what, we have no idea, but I strongly suspect the cat. Duke gets terrible hot spots and itchy sores on his chest and stomach. To keep the sores under control and help them heal, we give him a bath every few weeks and carefully remove the dead tissue so that Duke's skin can heal. It must hurt like crazy, but Duke never lets out a peep. It's as if he knows that we're only trying to help him.

—MICHAEL REICH
HELLERTOWN, PENNSYLVANIA
🐕 DUKE, 10

GRIFFEY HAS BATTLED TWO MEDICAL PROBLEMS, but he's handled it very well. When a pinched nerve in his neck made it too painful for him to move, Griffey allowed us to carry him and bring him to the vet for pain shots. And when a slipped disc forced his tail to go between his legs, Griffey dealt with it in his own way. Although his tail made it difficult for him to have a bowel movement, he would run across the yard until the poop finally came out. He needed prednisone and pain medication, but he never growled or stopped being his lovable self.

—CHAR LAVALETTE
RALEIGH, NORTH CAROLINA
🐕 GRIFFEY, BEAGLE, 8
🐕 RANDY, TERRIER MIX, 9

COLUMBO, a 10-year-old Basset Hound, must have been the father of a teenage girl in a previous life: He scrutinizes his owner's dates.

LISA ANSELL (OWNER)
BEVERLY HILLS, CALIFORNIA

LIVING ON A MILITARY BASE IN GERMANY, my husband and I went on a bike ride and took our dog Reilly with us. We were biking through the woods near where the soldiers train, and Reilly went running off. He ended up getting caught up in the security wire the soldiers string up. It's the kind with sharp spikes, is hard to see and is designed to catch the enemy if anyone is trying to sneak up on the soldiers' camp. Reilly went running right into it and got tangled, so the soldiers managed to catch themselves a dog. We had to cut the poor guy out!

—DERRITH MURPHY
BABENHAUSEN, GERMANY
REILLY, 1

• • • • • • • • •

WE USED TO TAKE SMITHERS walking up at the reservation. Greyhounds are not supposed to be off leash because they'll run away. But Smithers was too scared with a leash on (having been mistreated as a racing dog, he was scared of almost everything), so I'd let him walk right next to me, where he always stayed. Well, one hot afternoon, he saw a deer and took off. Four of us searched for an hour. Suddenly, we saw him. He stood looking at us for a second, and then collapsed. We ran back and got him into the car. Greyhounds overheat, and he was almost dead. The vet said his kidneys had failed, and he wasn't going to make it. But miraculously, he lived.

—MEG
MONTCLAIR, NEW JERSEY
SMITHERS, GREYHOUND, 3

BEAR, of Atlanta, Georgia, survived a policeman's bullet and much more.

ANNA KILINSKI (OWNER)

I ADOPTED CHOICEY AFTER HER PHOTO ran in the newspaper above a headline that said she and her eight three-week-old puppies would be put to sleep that day at the city shelter. It was an article about the importance of spaying and neutering. She was three years old then and had had 30 puppies. Her owner, tired of all those pups and not able to figure out the easy way to stop them, took her and the babies to the city shelter. As soon as I saw her photo, with her pleading eyes and terrified look, I knew I had to save them. I offered to foster them until the pups were old enough to be adopted. Having never had a puppy to care for by myself, it was quite an experience. At about nine weeks of age, the puppies were all adopted. Of course, I adopted Choicey.

—J.
DALLAS, TEXAS
🐕 CHOICEY, 15
🐕 MUFFIN, SHIH TZU-MALTESE MIX, 3

DUFFER HAD HIS LEG BROKEN IN TWO SPOTS. The vet told us to put him to sleep because he needed two surgeries to repair his leg. It would be expensive, and most people wouldn't want to pay for it. Fortunately, the University of Minnesota was able to operate on Duffer and he made a full recovery and lived a long, arthritis-free life.

—CINDY SCHWIE
ROSEVILLE, MINNESOTA
🐕 DUFFER, 15 🐕 ANNIE, 15, MIXED BREEDS

WHEN COLUMBO WAS SEVEN YEARS OLD, I saved his life. We were living at a rental house. One day, I left him in the backyard while I was at work. I checked the yard and it was secure, so I was very surprised when my landlady called me at work and said that Columbo was barking nonstop, but that she'd looked everywhere and could not find him. She said it sounded like he might be under the house. I rushed home, and when I got to the house I called his name. All I could hear was a faint bark. I started looking around the perimeter of the house to figure out where and how he got under. Eventually I found a tiny hole in the side of the house. I was able to squeeze through the hole into the pitch-black crawl space of the house, moving through cobwebs, rodents and everything else that lives in dirt. I finally found him and he had fallen down a six-foot ditch under the house. I immediately pushed myself down there. Next I had to figure out how I was going to bring him back up to safety. He weighs 70 pounds and I'm really small and don't have much upper-body strength. I called on all my superhuman strength, hoisted him up and got him out. He had a few cuts but he was alive and well.

—LISA ANSELL
BEVERLY HILLS, CALIFORNIA
🐕 COLUMBO, BASSET HOUND, 10

Bad Dog

They may be called Buddy, Tootsie, or Muffin on their tags, but their middle name is Trouble. These dogs must've earned an advanced degree at disobedience school to get into so much hot water so often. Oh, they know they've been bad. But they also seem to know they'll be forgiven—and they always are.

MY DOG WOULD STEAL MY BRA, panties, socks, nylons, shirt, or anything he could carry and put under the bed. I had to offer him hamburger treats to get my stuff back. It sometimes took me 25 extra minutes each morning to beg on my hands and knees, make the trades to retrieve my clothes, and get dressed for work!

—BABE BOOTH
LAKE OZARKS, MISSOURI
🐕 BLACKBERRI, MIXED BREED

• • • • • • • •

MY MOM'S FRIEND HAD A FEW HUGE AFGHANS (one of the dumbest dogs ever), and so she gave one to my mom. My parents left the dog home one day, and it chewed up my dad's antique kitchen table. I mean, it chewed off *an entire side.* That was the end of that dog; they gave it back.

—ANONYMOUS
DAVIE, FLORIDA

• • • • • • • •

ONE AFTERNOON WHILE I WAS AT WORK, Emma Blu decided to strip my bed. She didn't just take the comforter off and remove the sheets, but also all the pillows. Then she attacked the mattress. I walked into a pile of feathers, foam, filling, and fluff!

—HEIDI HENDERSON
KILLINGTON, VERMONT
🐕 EMMA BLU, 1 🐕 LOGAN, 1
🐕 SHASTA DELANEY, 5, BERNESE MOUNTAIN DOGS

DUFFER CHEWED THE CORNER of our son's playpen. When I turned the playpen around so no one could see the hole, he chewed the opposite corner! I think he wasn't too pleased with the addition of a sibling to the happy home that had previously featured only Duffer, my husband, and me.

> —CINDY SCHWIE
> ROSEVILLE, MINNESOTA
> 🐕 DUFFER, 15 🐕 ANNIE, 15, MIXED BREEDS

• • • • • • • •

I LIKE IT WHEN WE PLAY TUG-OF-WAR. But we can't play that much anymore because one dog takes the toy from the other and eats it.

> —COLE DRAPER, AGE 8
> DALLAS, TEXAS
> 🐕 CASEY, GOLDEN RETRIEVER, 13
> 🐕 DARBY, LABRADOR-POODLE MIX, 3

• • • • • • • •

ONE TIME, OUR DOG PULLED OVER the stroller with the baby still in it. The dog barely survived the aftermath. Another time, he messed in 11 different spots on our $5,000 oriental rug. We had to pay $300 to get it cleaned. Even the cleaners weren't hopeful when they saw it. Lucky for the dog, it all came out. He barely, and I mean *barely*, survived that one.

> —CLARE DAVIS
> MINNEAPOLIS, MINNESOTA
> 🐕 BARNABAS, MIXED BREED, 6

When we throw the ball, our dog runs and gets it. Then she gets wild and doesn't let you get the ball and we have to chase after her.

—SOPHIE ALFORD
DALLAS, TEXAS

OUR DOG DUKE LOVES TO PLAY with stuffed animals. Since our son was born last year, we've really tried to keep the baby's stuffed animals away from the dog, and vice versa. One day, I brought home a new stuffed duck for the baby. The baby had been playing with it, but I took him into another room and forgot the toy was on the floor. A few minutes later, my husband asked, "What's that quacking sound?" "Oops," I yelled and ran to the other room. There was Duke, duck toy in mouth, stuffing all around. That was one baby toy that quickly became a dog toy.

—JENNIFER REICH
HELLERTOWN, PENNSYLVANIA
🐕 DUKE, 10

Meet **DUFFER**, a big fan of lying in the back window of cars and open suitcases.

CINDY SCHWIE (OWNER)
ROSEVILLE, MINNESOTA

MY DOG HAS A BAD HABIT OF going outside and, when no one is looking, rolling around in poop. One time she did it and I gave her a bath. About an hour later, she needed another bath because she did it again!

—DEBBI SCHWARTZENFELD
BERKLEY, MICHIGAN
KALLI, 5

* * * * * * * *

WHENEVER LUCY BRINGS in something she shouldn't from outside, she holds her head high and races straight to her bed in the living room. One evening it was the same old story and I went over to rip what I thought was a stick out of her mouth. She was reluctant, but I fought her and won, only then realizing I was holding a rat carcass—bones and fur included.

—JENNIFER KRAMER
MINNEAPOLIS, MINNESOTA
LUCILLE BELLE, 1

* * * * * * * *

I DIDN'T KNOW HOW LONG my dog's tongue was until I took him to a pet store. We were standing in line when a little girl pet him on his back. My silly dog, in one motion, opened his mouth, pulled out his tongue, and licked her whole face. She was drenched. I was so embarrassed. From that moment on, every time I kiss Ali, I close his mouth.

—SCHENITA STEWART
GLENWOOD, ILLINOIS
ALI, AMERICAN STAFFORDSHIRE TERRIER, 3

MY DOG GETS INTO EVERYTHING. One night I came home, and my wood floors were covered in white powder. I had no idea what this powder was until I followed the trail of it into my kitchen, where a torn empty bag of flour sat near the cabinet. My dog had devoured the entire bag. The funny part, though, was that he drank a whole bowl of water when he finished eating. You know what you get when you mix flour and water, right? Paste. Yes, my dog had wheat paste stuck to his face for about a week after the incident.

—ANONYMOUS
LOS ANGELES, CALIFORNIA
ELMER, 4   MABEL, 4, BEAGLES

• • • • • • • • •

Hailey likes to chew the cables behind the TV when we are gone. We have that area blocked off now. She also chewed up my husband's eyeglasses. He was not too happy about that!

—HEATHER NELSON
PLYMOUTH, MINNESOTA
HAILEY, MIXED BREED, 1

ONE DAY MY HUSBAND AND I were outside working in our yard with our dog Duke. But Duke was being a bit of a pest, so we banished him to the house. He wasn't happy about it and sat at the sliding glass door, looking longingly at us. When we noticed his sad looks, Duke saluted us by raising his paw and flicking down the lock, locking us outside. Luckily, my husband had taken a key out with us, which we've done from that day forward.

—JENNIFER REICH
HELLERTOWN, PENNSYLVANIA
🐕 DUKE, 10

· · · · · · · · ·

BUSTER HAD SOME BAD HABITS when he first came to me. One of the things that's funny about Lhasas is that they shriek when they're upset or hurting. You can't tell when they have a splinter or a broken leg; they're very dramatic. Buster had been living with a woman who was herself a hypochondriac. He learned that if he lay on the bed and carried on, she would give him all kinds of attention. She thought he was sick all the time. The first time he started this with me, I just ignored him. He'd been checked out by a vet, and I knew there wasn't a darn thing wrong with him. I just said, "No, I'm not going to respond to that kind of whining and crying." Buster quickly changed his behavior.

—KATE MCGRAW
SANTA FE, NEW MEXICO
🐕 BUSTER, LHASA APSO, 8

My dog jumps on my bed when I'm at work. When I come home, he lies next to the bed, hoping I can't see the fur he left behind.

—SCHENITA
STEWART
GLENWOOD,
ILLINOIS
🐕 ALI,
AMERICAN
STAFFORDSHIRE
TERRIER, 3

MY WIFE COMPETES WITH MY DOGS in agility, which is essentially obstacle racing with dogs. Our dogs are completely food-motivated and one day, my wife was at a competition at a local park. The organization sponsoring the event was serving breakfast, buffet-style, on the picnic tables. My wife was out walking with one of the dogs and Mabel was tucked away in her crate. At least, that's what she thought until she heard someone scream, "There's a beagle in the bagels!" My wife, mortified, ran over to Mabel, and a startled Mabel, knowing that her time was near, immediately dove into the bagels to eat as much and as fast as she could. Well, this story was written up in our local newsletter and they were happy to report that, "no harm came to anyone who later had a bagel (there were only a few left), or to Mabel."

—ANONYMOUS
LOS ANGELES, CALIFORNIA
🐕 ELMER, 4 🐕 MABEL, 4, BEAGLES

• • • • • • • •

MY BOYFRIEND BOUGHT these "puppy pads" that look like giant Depends that you lay on the floor. They smell like dog urine, which, in theory, makes your dog want to pee on them. Mr. Bojangles missed that memo, however. Instead, he picks the pad up in his mouth and does laps around the house, then wraps himself up in it. Money well spent!

—KRISTEN HURD
TULSA, OKLAHOMA
🐕 MR. BOJANGLES, MINIATURE DACHSHUND

GOOD OLD SHOE

When he was younger, Tadpole was always escaping. He was like Houdini; he could open doors with his nose. One day he broke his outdoor leash and took off into the woods. I started chasing him, but he was gone. Then I noticed a tree that had been blown over. There was a big hole where the roots had been and it was full of shoes! Tadpole was famous for taking shoes; I used to warn people not to leave them around. All this time, I thought he was chewing them up but he was storing them in the woods. Some of them were mine, and some were my roommate's, but there were a bunch that I didn't recognize. He must have been stealing them from the neighbors when they left them outside! The funny thing is, he didn't take pairs, only single shoes. For him, I think it was this great game of hide-and-seek. He loved getting a reaction, which he did. At first I would be really mad, but then I'd buy a new pair of shoes and find the whole thing kind of amusing. When you love your dog, you can pretty much forgive anything.

—BRIAN CAROLLO
SIDNEY CENTER, NEW YORK
TADPOLE, ENGLISH-IRISH SETTER MIX, 16

HE ATE THE WHOLE THING

Five years ago my mom was going to do Thanksgiving dinner. She cooked up a storm all day long, including a 17-pound turkey that took eight hours to cook. When the turkey was done, she took it out of the oven and placed it on the kitchen counter to cool. At that point she realized she needed to make a final market run, and asked me to come along. We assumed the turkey was safe up on the kitchen counter because Columbo's got these pudgy, 6-inch legs and can't even jump. We came home from the store, opened the front door, and the first thing we see is a giant turkey carcass. Right then my mom started hyperventilating. Our guests were arriving in an hour and we had no turkey. We walked a bit farther into the house and from where we were we could see Columbo's legs and then we saw his stomach—it looked like the belly of a pregnant woman nine months along. My dog, whom I now call "Fat Boy Columbo," was able to jump his two front paws onto the chair that was by the phone that was next to the counter where the turkey was. He managed to knock the phone off the wall which then knocked the turkey onto the floor. My smart dog didn't eat for the next three days.

—LISA ANSELL
BEVERLY HILLS, CALIFORNIA
🐕 COLUMBO, BASSET HOUND, 10

BUTTONS WAS BIG AND GOOFY and a little neurotic. When I divorced, I was given the enormous pile of pillows we accumulated from our hippie days (we actually had furniture at this time, but hadn't gotten rid of the pillows). Having finally decided the time had come to weed out the musty and unwanted pillows (about 20 of the 40 or so in our collection), my second wife, Christina, and I bagged the "to go" pile and left the still-large mound of keepers in a relatively empty room in the center of the second floor. While we were out getting rid of the pillows we didn't want, Buttons proceeded to tear apart and shred every single one of the "keepers"! We came home to a foot-deep sea of stuffing that covered the entire room.

—BILL WHELAN
FREEPORT, MAINE
🐕 MAGGIE, COLLIE MIX, 14
🐕 BUTTONS, DALMATIAN, 4
🐕 SAM, LHASA APSO-POODLE MIX, 14

• • • • • • • • •

I HAVE THE ANSWER for how to cure a dog from barking in the house. Here's what you do: Get a big tin can, something large enough to put noisemakers in it. Load it with pennies or screws, anything that's metal and heavy. When the dog starts to bark, just shake the can. This makes Molly stop barking right away.

—ANONYMOUS
BIRMIMGHAM, ALABAMA
🐕 MOLLY, DALMATIAN, 10

SASSY IS A GREAT DOG, but the one thing that has given me the most problem is her desire to visit the neighbors and their little dogs. I've tried everything from scolding her, shutting her behind the fence and offering her a favorite treat, but she still wants to go for a visit. She and I have finally come to a compromise: She visits for just a minute and comes right back. It's an arrangement that two best friends can manage.

—DESSARINE MCNEILL
MAGNOLIA, ARKANSAS
SASSY, CHOW CHOW-GERMAN SHEPHERD MIX, 8
CUDDLES, 13

* * * * * * * *

MY HUSBAND AND I came home after being away for a couple of hours and noticed that our dog had shredded every piece of newspaper in the house. It was actually very impressive; it was hard to believe the shredding was done by a dog and not professionally by a large shredding machine because it was in very neat strips, entirely covering the first floor of my home.

—ANONYMOUS
TORONTO, CANADA
GREAT DANE

Weird Dog

There's dog behavior we understand, such as circling before lying down, or submissively turning belly-up before a pack leader. Then there's dog behavior for which there's absolutely no explanation: obsessively following the pool sweep; barking at a crack in the floor; collecting disgusting bits; chasing ghosts. Weird is the only word for it. Although our dogs may have their little quirks, we learn to live with their weirdness—and they learn to live with ours.

WHEN MY PAGER GOES OFF, my dog stops in his tracks
and freezes. He stands there in some kind of deep trance,
staring at one spot on the floor. You can call his name,
wave a biscuit in front of him, jump up and down, bang
on a table, or clap your hands; it won't break the spell.
The only thing that works is to pick him up and put him
down again. It's like he has to be reset.

—MARIE BALL
LINDENHURST, NEW YORK
🐕 BOCCI, 10 🐕 BELLA, 4

THE WEIRDEST THING my dog has ever done was fetch
something that I didn't throw. Sometimes, I may let her
run in the park, and she would run to me with a
stick, or old pop can in her mouth, salivating, as
if she did something wonderful. One time she even
ran to me with a Frisbee that belonged to someone else.

—BETH HARVEY
CHICAGO, ILLINOIS
🐕 ESSIE, SHEPHERD-SPANIEL-LAB MIX, 10

WHEN I ASK ALLY if she wants a tummy kiss, she rolls
over on her back and spreads her legs. Then she grabs
my head with her paws and forces my face down to her
stomach, way down there. She's just like a man; she tells
you exactly where she likes it!

—KATHLEEN SUE ROTTNER-PINK
LOS ANGELES, CALIFORNIA
🐕 ALLY, 4

SKI HAS A STUFFED RABBIT in a dress that he's had since he was six months old. He always treated it with the utmost care and never chewed it. But one night when he was about a year and half old, I heard this strange noise from where he was sitting. It was kind of like a combination of lips puckering and sheets tearing. I got up to see what was going on, and Ski had the little bunny's dress pulled up above her head, he had her legs spread open and was pulling the stuffing out from directly between her legs. I have no idea where he learned how to do that!

—LAURA CHAVERS
MANHATTAN BEACH, CALIFORNIA
🐕 SKI, 10
🐕 JAKE, MIXED BREED, 2

· · · · · · · · ·

MOST PEOPLE ARE ADDICTED to something: love, sweets, cigarettes, alcohol. Jaxon is addicted to water. He loves it! I actually have to limit his water intake throughout the day because he drinks it too quickly and gets sick. As soon as the bath water starts to run he gets all jazzed up and tries to jump in the tub. He stands there waiting for any drips or dribbles that he might be able to lick up. I took him to a beach for the first time a few weeks ago and he dove right into the water. In Central Park he jumped straight into the lake and took a swim in the fountain. Is there such a thing as Waters Anonymous?

—KELLI BRISBANE
NEW YORK, NEW YORK
🐕 JAXON, YORKIE, 1

BOCCI needs to be "reset" every time his owner's pager goes off.

MARIE BALL (OWNER)
LINDENHURST, NEW YORK

MAX IS VERY JEALOUS. If you hug someone else, he starts whining. If you get a little bit more intimate, he starts moaning. Any kind of embrace or affection sets him off. He wants to be part of it, or he wants people to separate. Needless to say, nothing ever happens in our bedroom if Max is around.

> —YVONNE
> CHERRY HILL, NEW JERSEY
> 🐕 SNICKERS, 11 🐕 MAX, 3

* * * * * * * *

MUFFIN IS SLIGHTLY OBSESSIVE-COMPULSIVE. Whenever we go to my father's house, Muffin runs out to his pool and sits there and watches the pool sweep go around. She literally sits there for hours just following it around the pool.

> —SHARON KRUGER
> LOS ANGELES, CALIFORNIA
> 🐕 LIBBY, 3
> 🐕 MUFFIN, HAVANESE, 4

* * * * * * * *

MY DOG IS A SHELTIE, and they were bred to herd sheep. Lacking a convenient herd of sheep, Casey makes up for it by herding people. Whenever we have a party, she runs frantically from room to room, trying to get everyone in the same room. When everyone finally does end up in one room, she collapses and falls asleep, apparently happy that the herd is safe.

> —SHAROLYN WIEBE
> VANCOUVER, CANADA
> 🐕 CASEY, SHELTIE, 9

Miles tries to jump in the bathtub every time I take a bath, which is pretty strange, especially since he doesn't like his own bath.

> —PAULA
> INGLEWOOD,
> CALIFORNIA
> 🐕 MILES,
> MALTEPOO, 2

DOLCE ENJOYS COMBING PEOPLE'S HAIR and will do it for hours. He actually looks like a tiny barber running the nails of his two front paws through anyone's hair. If you lie down on the ground and are anywhere near him, and if your hair needs brushing, expect him to fully pamper you.

—ANONYMOUS
LOS ANGELES, CALIFORNIA
🐕 DOLCE, SHIH TZU

* * * * * * * *

My dog will only eat one type of food, Alpo. If I put anything else in front of her, she'll turn her bowl over, or run to the back porch and moan.

—BETH HARVEY
CHICAGO, ILLINOIS
🐕 ESSIE, SHEPHERD-SPANIEL-LAB MIX, 10

* * * * * * * *

MY DOG LIKES GRAPES. He'll pick them up in his mouth and take them into the living room and drop them on the ground. He won't actually eat them for about 30 minutes.

—ANDREA WIESE
CHESTERTON, INDIANA
🐕 JACKSON, MIXED BREED, 4

JAXON, a Yorkshire Terrier, is addicted to water, according to his owner.

KELLI BRISBANE (OWNER)
NEW YORK, NEW YORK

WHEN OUR FIRST SON WAS BORN, my wife changed his dirty diaper on the floor and got up to get more wipes to clean him up. When she returned, the diaper was still there, but its contents were gone! She figured out what happened when she saw the dog nearby, licking her chops. Needless to say, we don't leave diapers on the floor anymore.

—C.A.
CINCINNATI, OHIO
🐕 SYDNEY, SHEPHERD MIX, 8

• • • • • • • •

I LOVED TO WATCH STANLEY be a spectator when the kids had arguments or pillow fights. To get out of the line of fire, he would hide under the desk; peeking out, motionless, with his eyes and nose glued to the goings-on. I guess he was afraid he would be hit with a toy or a pillow if he were detected, so only his eyes moved during the action.

—PAM DUGGINS
ST. LOUIS, MISSOURI
🐕 STANLEY, COCKER SPANIEL-GOLDEN RETRIEVER MIX

• • • • • • • •

THE SECOND I'VE HAD A BATH or shower—or even a pedicure—Lucy knows it. She immediately proceeds to lick my legs and though I know she's merely obsessed with the scents and lotions, I feel as if she's thinking the conventional bath is totally unsatisfactory.

—JENNIFER KRAMER
MINNEAPOLIS, MINNESOTA
🐕 LUCILLE BELLE, 1

Odd Fellows

We humans think dogs are our best friends. Our dogs, however, may prefer companions of a very different stripe.
Or spot. Or species. The dogs in this chapter (and their pals) display
a heartwarming openness to diversity, an ability to just get along
together, and constant proof that the language of friendship is,
indeed, universal.

MILES'S BEST FRIEND IS A PARROT named Sweetie. At first I was worried that Miles would try to attack or eat Sweetie, but he actually guards him. There's a cat that roams around the neighborhood: Miles makes a lot of noise when the cat comes around, so Sweetie is well protected.

—PAULA
INGLEWOOD, CALIFORNIA
🐕 MILES, MALTEPOO, 2

· · · · · · · · ·

BLACKBERRI HAD A VERY UNUSUAL FRIENDSHIP with our tame white dove, Crisco. When they were playing in the yard, Crisco would fly up and land on Blackberri, riding him bareback. Blackberri loved it—he would strut around the yard, proudly showing off his fine feathered friend.

—BABE BOOTH
LAKE OZARKS, MISSOURI
🐕 BLACKBERRI, MIXED BREED

· · · · · · · · ·

MY DOG HAS A STRANGE RELATIONSHIP with the raccoons in my neighborhood. My dog's fur is grey, just like a raccoon. He's also small like them so I really think that the raccoons believe that he is one of them and they are trying to rescue him from my house. When I hear Max barking I go outside, and there are usually a ton of raccoons just standing on my deck on their hind legs. It's as if they are just waiting to take Max with them.

—JULIE
BEVERLY HILLS, CALIFORNIA
🐕 MAX, SHIH TZU-POODLE MIX, 4

LUCY, an Australian Cattle Dog, and FRANKIE, a Westie,
are inseparable.

JOHN (OWNER)
LOS ANGELES, CALIFORNIA

NOT TOO LONG AFTER I GOT MY DOG Bailey, a cat showed up in my yard and never left. I was really worried about how they would get along since they weren't raised together, but they adjusted to each other pretty quickly. I would find them sleeping nose-to-nose—and that was after only two months of being together. And God forbid I should take Bailey for a walk without Blinky. Bailey goes crazy, tearing around the house, running from door to door, crying. Blinky trots along behind us, and if he falls behind, Bailey stops, turns around and looks for him. If other dogs bother Blinky, Bailey goes nuts trying to defend him! People always stop me and ask how I trained a cat to take walks. I didn't. It's all about being with Bailey. I'm sure they talk to each other. I just wish I knew what they're saying.

—PETER D. GIBBONS
N. MASSAPEQUA, NEW YORK
🐕 BAILEY, GOLDEN RETRIEVER-RESCUE DOG, 6
🐕 HANNAH, GOLDEN RETRIEVER, 13

• • • • • • • •

OUR DOG HAS A NIGHTLY TRADITION. Each evening, he chases the same squirrel around our yard. And, each evening, the squirrel escapes his wrath, scoots up a tree, and laughs at him. Still, the dog never gives up. Every single night, he chases that squirrel, and said squirrel always ends up laughing at him.

—CLARE DAVIS
MINNEAPOLIS, MINNESOTA
🐕 BARNABAS, MIXED BREED, 6

I HAVE GOATS NAMED ROSEBUD and Sweet Pea in a pen in my backyard. They've been with me since before I had my dogs. Every morning, my dogs go outside and "fence fight" with the goats. The goats smash the fence while the dogs run around on the opposite side. They love playing with each other so much that the fences are bent from the goats punching the fence.

—BARBARA LOMBARD
SIMI VALLEY, CALIFORNIA
🐕 HEMI, 3 🐕 T.J., 2
🐕 TURBO, 8, SHELTIES

• • • • • • • •

MY NEIGHBOR HAD A HORSE that was 40 years old, which is pretty old for a horse. She used to bring him over to graze in our yard because we had a big back yard with all sorts of wild oats. When the horse was in our yard, we didn't let the dogs out; a horse can do some pretty serious damage to a dog, and my dogs hadn't ever been around horses before. One day, Wylie got out while the horse was over, and my neighbor and I said, "Let's just see what happens." It was so adorable: Wylie looked at the horse, then the horse looked at him. Their eyes met, they kind of sized each other up, and Wylie ran and got one of his squeaky balls and ran over to the horse with it. He gave the horse a look that said, "Wanna play?" The horse was like, "Hey bud, just leave me alone."

—CHRISTY CONN
THOUSAND OAKS, CALIFORNIA
🐕 KATY, 1 🐕 WYLIE, 4, SHELTIES

Buster is an incredible fly catcher and considers them a tasty treat. No fly, no matter how quick or small, is safe from his tummy.

—NIKI FRIEDMAN
NEW YORK,
NEW YORK
🐕 BUSTER, 4

MY DOG, JILL, LOVED TO CHASE CHIPMUNKS, but they were so little and fast and she was so big that it was pretty funny. After a few circles around the yard, the chipmunk ran right at her and between her front legs. Jill had been running hard, and put her head down between her legs to try and catch the chipmunk, and somersaulted head over heels. Jill got up, sat there thinking for a few minutes and then started to chase the chipmunk again. And the same thing happened!

—PAT
ROSEVILLE, MINNESOTA
🐕 JILL, GERMAN SHEPHERD, 5
🐕 PUPPY, 3 🐕 MAGGIE, 11, MIXED BREEDS

* * * * * * * *

ABOUT A YEAR AGO we bought a white bunny rabbit for my son. For the first few months we kept him in his cage, with supervised walks around the house. During those walks, Barkly was kept in the kitchen. One day Barkly decided he was going to knock down the fence that kept him in the kitchen and charge our bunny. Bunny freaked out for a second, but then Barkly just started licking him. Now Barkly and Bunny roam the house freely and sleep in the same bed.

—KRISTI
LOS ANGELES, CALIFORNIA
🐕 BARKLY, JACK RUSSELL, 4

TEMPE is a five-year-old Australian Cattle Dog.

WHEN OUR DOG SOPHIE was still pretty young, something happened that changed her forever. I saw her in the backyard, pushing her nose into something on the ground, moving it around. When I investigated, I saw that it was a baby squirrel that had apparently fallen from the tree. Sophie was trying to play with it, but I was sure she would kill it; she's not exactly subtle. So I took her inside, very much against her will. By the time I went back out, the mother squirrel had come down, picked up the baby, and was running off with it. From that moment on, Sophie has been obsessed with squirrels. Whenever she's outside, it's all she looks for; whenever we let her off the leash, she runs for the nearest tree and looks for squirrels. One time, she was in the car with me, and when a squirrel crossed the road in front of us, she tried to leap through the windshield to get it. It's as if she's looking for that squirrel pal she met when she was young. She's convinced that every squirrel she sees might be the one. Either that, or she just wants to finally kill a squirrel.

—J.A.
ATLANTA, GEORGIA
🐕 SOPHIE, LABRADOR-AUSTRALIAN SHEPHERD MIX, 2
🐕 CLIFTON, MIXED BREED, 10

OINK, MY GUINEA PIG, lives in a fish tank that is uncovered. A couple of times a day he comes out for playtime. While he's resting in his tank, my dog Sparks stands guard and stares at him. When he comes out to play he's either on the sofa or on the bed and Sparks basically runs around like a maniac in the same direction as Oink. They don't touch but they definitely play.

—CHIP MASON
LOS ANGELES, CALIFORNIA
SPARKS, GOLDEN RETRIEVER, 6

I HAVE A FOUR-YEAR-OLD FEMALE BOXER named Bella. I also have a three-year-old pot-bellied pig named Gibson. Bella enjoys tormenting Gibson by chasing him around in tight circles as fast as she can until she gets tired or I get tired of it. Being the token big sister, she is also very protective of her little brother. One day while on a walk with the pig and the dog, an unleashed dog walked up to investigate my stub-nosed, 50-plus pounds of walking ham. Bella immediately positioned herself in between Gibson and the strange dog. The new dog, completely undeterred, crouched below Bella in order to get a better view of the pig. Bella turned her head completely around and under her body in order to keep an eye on things. This was a picture that would have sold millions of greeting cards! To this day, dog and pig still share a kennel and fight over food on a daily basis.

—DAVE HUDSON
ST. CLOUD, MINNESOTA
BELLA, BOXER, 4

KATY, MY SHELTIE, loves my niece's two ferrets. She doesn't quite know what they are and I think at first greeting she wanted to eat them. But after a few minutes of sniffing she realized they are just another kind of animal. We take the ferrets out all the time to play with Katie. They run around the room and play hide-and-seek. They'll hide behind something then stick their little heads out and Katy will run to one corner where she saw the ferret go and the ferret will come around, bite Katy on the butt and then run away. It's just adorable.

—CHRISTY CONN
THOUSAND OAKS, CALIFORNIA
🐾 KATY, 1 🐾 WYLIE, 4, SHELTIES

Almost Human?

I t seems almost inevitable: Dog lives with human; dog becomes a bit human. We can all identify ways in which our dogs act like humans—like us, in fact! But are we as sharp at noticing all the ways in which we become more like our dogs? Think about it next time you go out to howl at the moon.

MY STEP-DOG, FOOLISH, seems to rely on his vision more than his nose; a very human thing to do. Once, when he was staying with me, I discovered him in a standoff with a tea cozy. The tea cozy had a photo-transfer image of a cat on it, and was propped up on the windowsill. Foolish was planted in front of this object, growling and baring his teeth. He truly did not know it wasn't a real cat.

—N.
BROOKLYN, NEW YORK

• • • • • • • • •

MY DOG MUFFIN wants to be just like me. She's eager to learn how to do everything I do and once she figures it out she becomes independent and refuses help from me. I used to clean her eyes, but now she can tell when I'm about to do it and pulls back in order to do it herself. She even cleans her sister's eyes. After watching me clean up her potty pads, she decided she would also take this chore into her own hands. After she goes to the bath-room, she proceeds to fold up her pad using her nose. These are not easy tasks for a dog.

—SHARON KRUGER
LOS ANGELES, CALIFORNIA
🐕 LIBBY, 3
🐕 MUFFIN, HAVANESE, 4

REX, an Akita-Border Collie mix from California, shows off a lovely collar.

DENISE FLECK (OWNER)
SHADOW HILLS, CALIFORNIA

MY BOYFRIEND AND I travel extensively. He has a private plane, which means we get to take our dogs on vacation. The first time we took Ski on the plane, he jumped up onto a seat, made himself comfortable, and looked out the window through the entire flight. Ski is our child, so why would we make him sit anywhere else?

—LAURA CHAVERS
MANHATTAN BEACH, CALIFORNIA
🐕 SKI, 10
🐕 JAKE, MIXED BREED, 2

* * * * * * * * *

It's hard not to apply human character- istics to dogs. Sometimes I think my dog knows this and plays with my mind.

—RANA KOLL-MANDEL
GARRETT PARK, MARYLAND
🐕 *BRISKET, 60% BEAGLE 40% CHICKEN, 3*

* * * * * * * * *

WE TRIED FEEDING SHANG DOG FOOD, but he thought he was one of us. When we would be at the dinner table eating rib tips, pork chops, or chicken wings, he would just salivate until we gave him something. I just couldn't resist him. So we got rid of the dog food.

—RUBEN REEVES
CHICAGO, ILLINOIS
🐕 SHANG, MIXED BREED, 2

MAGGIE IS THE OUTFIT-WEARING PRINCESS, who many refer to as a pocket dog: quite small, with large eyes and a little pink tongue that sticks out. Maggie is the kind of dog who refuses to go on walks, insisting she be carried in her tote bag. She likes to wear little shirts and sweaters; it makes her feel secure. Dog food disgusts her, so I have to cook everything from scratch. Hamburgers bring out a fierce appetite in her, and she will let out little barks, telling you to share!

—ANONYMOUS
LOS ANGELES, CALIFORNIA
🐕 MAGGIE, 4 🐕 MOZZY, 3, CHIHUAHUAS

* * * * * * * *

I DIDN'T MIND MY DOG sleeping on the bottom of my bed or on the floor beside my bed, but Maggie always wanted to move up and sleep right next to me. One time, my friend Doris, came to visit and stayed overnight. In the morning, I looked around for Maggie to let her out but could not find her. I went upstairs and there she was, happily tucked under the covers with her head on the pillow next to Doris. I whispered, "Maggie," and she opened her eyes and looked at me shamefacedly—and then turned over and went to sleep again.

—PAT
ROSEVILLE, MINNESOTA
🐕 JILL, GERMAN SHEPHERD, 5
🐕 PUPPY, 3 🐕 MAGGIE, 11, MIXED BREEDS

Ski talks. When he wants something, he says "Mommy." I always say I'm his mommy, so I think he learned it that way.

—LAURA CHAVERS
MANHATTAN BEACH, CALIFORNIA
🐕 SKI, 10
🐕 JAKE, MIXED BREED, 2

SOMETIMES I WOULD LET COCO sleep in the room with me, but he would snore at night. One time, I thought it was my mother in the other room until I looked on the floor and saw Coco sleeping like an old man.

—TINELL WILLIAMS
LITTLE ROCK, ILLINOIS
🐕 COCO, PIT BULL, 3

. . . .

OUR DOG HAS A GIRLFRIEND NAMED EMMA, another Golden Retriever. She lives four houses down from ours. They sniff and play. When he was young, my dog would cry if we didn't go by to say hello to Emma. Now, they are older; Boomer is eight, and he barely sniffs when he sees her. He can't be bothered. They went from being hot and heavy to barely saying hi. They're like an old married couple.

—ANONYMOUS
NEW CITY, NEW YORK
🐕 BOOMER, GOLDEN RETRIEVER, 8

. . . .

MY DOG SITS ON HIS BENCH and people-watches out the window; he's always trying to get into the driver's seat of the car; he watched the entire O.J. Simpson trial, and I thought he was going to riot at the end. And he drinks Pepsi when we allow it.

—JOHN FOCKE
MARQUETTE, MICHIGAN
🐕 JED, MIXED BREED, 12

BRANDI is a Shetland Sheepdog from California.

IAN LONG (OWNER)
RANCHO SANTA MARGARITA, CALIFORNIA

WHEN I YELL FOR MY HUSBAND AND KIDS to come for dinner, Kirbie runs like he is one of kids. He jumps up on my husband, Mike's, chair before Mike gets there and stands on his back legs, while his little front legs are resting on the table. Kirbie looks at me like, "What's for dinner, Mom?" He has this little smirk on his face and looks so eager for dinner. It's hilarious.

—ALICE OLSON
STILLWATER, MINNESOTA
KIRBIE, YORKSHIRE TERRIER, 5

MAX LIKES SITTING in the front section of the shopping cart, in the child's seat. And he's very well behaved. I was once in the checkout line with him sitting in the cart, and there was a woman with a four-year-old child, having one of those nightmare moments. She looked at me and said, "Your dog is better behaved than my child."

—JULIE
BEVERLY HILLS, CALIFORNIA
MAX, SHIH TZU-POODLE MIX, 4

ALLY'S BEST FRIEND IS MY NEIGHBOR'S DOG, Sophie. Sophie and Ally love to French kiss. Ally opens her mouth and Sophie sticks her tongue in it. They're lesbians, and we fully support it!

—KATHLEEN SUE ROTTNER-PINK
LOS ANGELES, CALIFORNIA
ALLY, 4

WE CONSIDER LULU TO BE HUMAN because we can see every emotion register on her face with complete clarity. It really makes leaving her alone very tough. We had to develop a heart of stone to close the door on that face every day, but coming home makes us feel so loved. She hurls her body against us and whimpers and yelps with glee. Her face peels back with an enormous smile and her ears become plastered against her head. She also has an "I love you" breathing pattern. When I hug her and say "good girl" in a gentle voice, she leans into me really hard and breathes a little shuddering, cheek-flapping sigh. We call it the I-Love-You breath.

—MARISKA VAN AALST
EMMAUS, PENNSYLVANIA
🐕 LULU, LABRADOR, 7

ON THEIR BIRTHDAYS, my dogs get a vanilla cupcake with a candle and they wear hats. They know when it's a birthday and they jump up into the chairs to celebrate.

—K.P.
TRUMBULL, CONNECTICUT
🐕 SOFT-COATED WHEATEN TERRIERS

KEA IS LIKE A PERSON. We wake up in the morning and kiss each other. She slides out of bed and we walk out of the bedroom together. I scratch my head, she scratches herself; she goes out to pee and I use the bathroom. Then, we eat breakfast together and just hang out before I have to go to work.

—SUE
ENCINO, CALIFORNIA
🐕 KEA LUCILLE, MIXED BREED, 11

Dog's Favorite Things

Raindrops on roses—maybe. Whiskers on kittens—definitely not. A dog's favorite things most likely resemble a tennis ball, although any objects in the soft, flying, smelly, squeaky, or tasty categories will certainly qualify. For many dogs, a favorite thing is something to do—ride in a car (but not to the vet or groomer), chase a ball, or snuggle up to a favorite human.

OZZIE'S OBSESSED WITH ANY BALL. He just has to have any ball that crosses his path. If he drops it, it means he wants you to throw it. He won't let it go until he's ready. And if you won't throw it he'll just walk around with it in his mouth all day.

—CHARLENE VALDEZ
SIMI VALLEY, CALIFORNIA
🐕 OZZIE, KEESHOND, 2
🐕 DR. PEPPER, DALMATIAN, 9

REILLY'S FAVORITE GAME WAS TETHERBALL. We used to go up to the grade school near our house and play all the time with him. All you had to do was hit the ball and get it spinning around the post, and Reilly would jump up and hit the ball with his nose. People would always stop to look at a dog playing tetherball!

—DERRITH MURPHY
BABENHAUSEN, GERMANY
🐕 REILLY, 1

LUCY LOVES CHEESE, oranges, broccoli, green beans, apples, eggs, oatmeal, potatoes, and lots of lettuce. Of course, she totally loves biscuits too. We have a ceramic cookie jar shaped like a dog, and she sits with her nose to the nose of the jar and then pushes it a little bit. We call it praying to the biscuit god.

—MILA CAPONE
SEAFORD, NEW YORK
🐕 LUCY, SHEPHERD-DOBERMAN MIX, 7

If you're playing catch with a Frisbee and JJ is around, he's likely to steal the flying disc mid-flight.

JOANNE (OWNER)
ST. PAUL, MINNESOTA

PRISSY HAS A WHITE, FLUFFY BLANKET that she holds between her paws and nurses every night before she goes to sleep. She drags it everywhere with her and no one is allowed to touch it. I have to sneak it into the laundry to be washed.

—DEBBIE
RINGGOLD, GEORGIA
🐕 PRISSY, AMERICAN ESKIMO, 1
🐕 GOLD, 12 🐕 SIMBA, 1, YELLOW LABS
🐕 COCOA, CHOCOLATE LAB, 1

• • • • • • • •

WE BUY BOOMER SPECIAL GIFTS every Christmas. Usually, my wife buys him a stuffed, fleece bone with a squeaker in it. He rips it to shreds, shaking his head, flinging all the foam around the room, until he gets the squeaker out. Then he stops. That's all he wants; to get that squeaker out.

—NICK
NEW CITY, NEW YORK
🐕 BOOMER, 8

• • • • • • • •

LULU LOVES MY SLIPPERS. She never shreds them but she loves to get them in her mouth and shake her head. When I wake up in the morning, I might have slippers or I might not have slippers. One or two might be out the doggie door. I'm just happy that she doesn't destroy them.

—CLAIRE MICHAELS
CANOGA PARK, CALIFORNIA
🐕 LULU, KEESHOND, 2

BUT THEY'RE GREAT FOR DETERRING BURGLARS …

The worst dog toys are the ones that you will invariably step on in the hallway on your way to the bathroom in the dark. Those are the ones with the hard edges or points that are sure to find the soft spots on the bottoms of your feet. It only took a couple of times of that happening to me before I started to wear my slippers anytime I was walking anywhere in the house in the dark.

—ANONYMOUS
STRONGSVILLE, OHIO
COLLIE, 2

FOUR WHEELS AND A TAIL

MOLLY IS A FABULOUS CAR DOG. She'll sit on the seat, very regal and dignified, just like "Driving Miss Daisy."

—ANONYMOUS
BIRMIMGHAM, ALABAMA
🐕 MOLLY, DALMATIAN, 10

• • • • • • • •

JAKE IS PART GREAT DANE. He likes to ride in the car, but he needs to stand like surfer boy on the center consul. He's so big, though, that when he's on the console his head hits the ceiling. My boyfriend recently got a new car. Every time we got in the car the back windshield wiper would be on and we couldn't figure out why. One day we discovered that the control button was on the ceiling of the car; Jake's head was pressing on it.

—LAURA CHAVERS
MANHATTAN BEACH, CALIFORNIA
🐕 SKI, 10
🐕 JAKE, MIXED BREED, 2

• • • • • • • •

EVERY TIME WE TOOK MY GREAT DANE IN THE CAR, it looked like a Marmaduke cartoon strip. She'd literally push us off the seats and stretch out in the back.

—ANDREA
TORONTO, CANADA
🐕 GREAT DANE

This Sheltie named AXEL jumps into his owner's arms every time she comes home.

GROOM AND DOOM

I MADE THE MISTAKE OF SAYING how our dog needed a haircut in front of my five-year-old son. When I wasn't looking, he took out scissors and chopped the dog. Luckily, he just got fur; no skin or eyeballs. But boy, was that one ugly dog.

—DEKE
SAN DIEGO, CALIFORNIA
🐕 MIXED BREED, 8

IF YOUR DOG IS LIKE OUR MUTT, don't put yourself through the torture of attempting baths. We take him to the pet salon about every three months for a bath, nails clipped and ears cleaned. It only costs $20 and it is well worth it. The dog would just freak out at home any time we tried to do it ourselves.

—CANDACE MISTELLI
BOARDMAN, OHIO
🐕 MIXED BREED, 2

SAM DREADS GOING TO THE VET. He actually starts talking to you in the car when you're getting close to the vet (he knows; he always knows!) and he paces and cries when we're in the waiting room. There doesn't seem to be any way to make this less of an ordeal for him.

—HUNTER
HUDSON VALLEY, NEW YORK
🐕 SAM

• • • • • • • • •

MY HUSBAND AND I HAD A TERRIBLE TIME clipping the dog's nails. He would fight us every step of the way. Then I found a way to make it much less painful for all of us. While my hubby is doing the clipping I distract the dog by putting peanut butter on my hand and letting the dog lick it off. The dog gets so involved with the food that it doesn't notice the clipping.

—TERRY DEL GRECO
FLORENCE, KENTUCKY
🐕 SPANIEL, 6

MY DOG, NEVER, TOLERATES OUR WALKS, because at the end of the walk she gets to stop by McDonald's and have a cheeseburger. She has them hold the pickles, though, because she doesn't like them. She can actually recognize the golden arches.

—H.O.
EVERETT, WASHINGTON
NEVER

• • • • • • • •

HAILEY HAS THIS STUFFED TOY TURKEY that she loves to play with. It's her very first toy; the breeder sent it home with her. She absolutely loves to play fetch with it. Of course when we brought it home, it was intact; but now, it doesn't even have any stuffing left in it, so when you throw it, it doesn't go very far. But, I don't dare throw it away because she knows this toy by its name. When we say to her, "Hailey, where's your turkey?" she will race around until she finds it.

—HEATHER NELSON
PLYMOUTH, MINNESOTA
HAILEY, MIXED BREED, 1

• • • • • • • •

LOUIE LOVES STUFFED ANIMALS, so I go to thrift stores to buy them. Right now he has a bunny rabbit about two feet long that I bought for $1.25. It'll take him about half a year to chew it up.

—LESLIE
MINNEAPOLIS, MINNESOTA
LOUIE, BOXER-ENGLISH SPRINGER SPANIEL MIX, 3

KIDS' BEST FRIEND

MY FAVORITE THING IS WHEN MY DOGS SLEEP WITH ME, because I get to cuddle them and spend time with them.

—JOSEY ALLEN
ATLANTA, GEORGIA
🐕 SOPHIE, 2 🐕 CLIFTON, 10

• • • • • • • •

LADDIE USED TO HELP ME GET READY FOR BED. He would pull off one sock and then he would pull off the other sock, and then he would pull my pants off. It was so fun! I wish he could still do it, but he's older now and his teeth might fall out.

—SARINA ELIZABETH STEVRALIA
EASTON, PENNSYLVANIA
🐕 LADDIE

OZZIE, a Keeshond, and a little friend, with one of Ozzie's favorite things—a tennis ball.

CHARLENE VALDEZ (OWNER)
SIMI VALLEY, CALIFORNIA

MUFFIN LOVES PEANUT BUTTER JARS. She chews on them, making sure to peel any paper labels off the jars. But her favorite thing to do with plastic jars is to push them around the floor or yard, growling all the while. She's really a smart little dog, but you wouldn't know it when she's chasing her peanut butter jar around!

—J.
DALLAS, TEXAS
🐕 CHOICEY, 15
🐕 MUFFIN, SHIH TZU-MALTESE MIX, 3

. . . .

SPIRIT'S FAVORITE THING is Iams dental treats. She sees me get the bag down from the top of the refrigerator, starts bouncing around in tight circles, and then will plant herself as close to me as she can be. She takes the treat, runs all over the living room (doing laps, I call it) throwing the treat up to herself, dropping it, running away from it and coming back to it. When she tires of playing with it, she will go under the dining room table and eat it.

—TRACY LEE ALLEN
FREDERICK, MARYLAND
🐕 SPIRIT, ENGLISH SPRINGER SPANIEL, 2

. . . .

BUSTER LOVES MY TENNIS SHOES. When I leave for work he gets my tennis shoes, brings them downstairs, and sits there with his head on my tennis shoes until I come home.

—TERRI BRINK
SANTA CLARITA, CALIFORNIA
🐕 BUSTER, 4 🐕 KODA, 3, AUSTRALIAN SHEPHERDS

SKYE'S FAVORITE TOY IS A HUGE TEDDY BEAR that sits on the floor. Skye likes to curl up and sleep on it; sometimes she likes to wrestle with it, and sometimes she likes to hump it.

—CAROL CURTISS
LAKE ELSINORE, CALIFORNIA
SKYE, 5 FAITH, 3
ALEX, 7, SHELTIES

* * * * * * * *

JJ LOVES TO PLAY FRISBEE. But rather than run out and fetch it from us, he prefers to stand between two people who are playing, then jump up and steal the Frisbee out of the air. It never fails to draw a laugh from the people around us.

—JOANNE
ST. PAUL, MINNESOTA
JJ, MIXED BREED, 2

* * * * * * * *

OUR DOG DIGS FOR ROCKS and then throws them in the pool. My husband scuba dives. One day, when he was in the pool practicing, the dog lay by the side of the pool and barked until he got every rock out of the pool. After we carted the rocks away, she would go get more and toss them in the pool again.

—TERI THOMPSON
SIMI VALLEY, CALIFORNIA
FAYTH, BORDER COLLIE, 3
AXEL, SHELTIE, 1

What We Do for Love

There's always a bump in the road, they say. Our dogs take care of us in so many ways that when the tables turn, we go to extraordinary lengths to return the favor. Others may view the undertaking as excessive; to us, it's only natural. We do it for love; that's what commitment means.

WHEN TRACY NEEDED KNEE SURGERY, my wife and I didn't think twice about it. We lived in a two-story house and Tracy always slept upstairs with us. After she had her surgery she couldn't walk up the stairs, so we made her a great bed of pillows downstairs and took turns sleeping with her on alternating nights.

—MALCOLM
LOS ANGELES, CALIFORNIA
🐕 CINDY, 7 🐕 TRACY, 10, BOXERS

• • • • • • • • •

MY DOG JAKE WAS EPILEPTIC. He'd have grand mal seizures about once a month, in clusters. It got to the point when, in the middle of a weeknight, before a big day of work, we'd have to rush him to the emergency vet so they could put him on a valium I.V. drip. I never thought twice about the cost of doing it, or how the lack of sleep would affect me the next day. Jake needed help. He would have died without it. To entertain myself on those after-midnight drives to the vet, I'd do something else for Jake that I've never done for anyone else: I wrote the words to a country song about him. I don't listen to that kind of music, but it seemed fitting—any tragic story about a dog deserves a country song.

—J.W.A.
ATLANTA, GEORGIA
🐕 JAKE, AUSTRALIAN SHEPHERD, 8

ONE DAY I DISCOVERED BLOOD in Frankie's urine and I rushed him over to the emergency room. The doctors didn't know what it was at first, but after several tests, they determined that he had bladder cancer. Bladder cancer is usually a death sentence for a dog, but we were determined to fight it. With the right care they can live out their natural life. Surgery cut out most of the cancer. After his surgery he went on chemotherapy and several other treatments. I'm at the vet's office at least three times a week, but it's worth it because my wife and I don't have children.

—JOHN
LOS ANGELES, CALIFORNIA
🐕 FRANK, WESTIE, 14
🐕 LUCY, AUSTRALIAN CATTLE DOG, 12

I HELPED MY DOG ALEX recover from complete paralysis. He did something to the second vertebrae of his neck that completely paralyzed him. He went through steroid treatment and he had some pills for a while, but I also used hydrotherapy and massage. I nursed him back to health and he was able to compete in agility and achieve Master Agility Champion, which is the highest title you can get in AKC agility. After this happened, people came up to me to ask if this was the miracle dog, and I would say, "Yes, this is Alex, my miracle dog."

—CAROL CURTISS
LAKE ELSINORE, CALIFORNIA
🐕 SKYE, 5 🐕 FAITH, 3
🐕 ALEX, 7, SHELTIES

ONE TIME WHEN DAISY was about nine months, we discovered that she had eaten a Mancala game piece—one of those little glass-flattened marbles. I called the vet ' and they were afraid that since Daisy was still such a little puppy it wouldn't pass. The vet said maybe it would show up on an X-ray, and then we'd have to take her to the university, and that would be $1,000 just to walk in. But what's the alternative? We were not going to let her die. But then I talked to another vet who said we could use hydrogen peroxide to get her to vomit. So we stuck two syringes-full down her throat. She vomited right away and there was the Mancala piece.

—SIDNEY
MINNEAPOLIS, MINNESOTA
🐕 DAISY, YORKSHIRE TERRIER, 1

I bathe Lil Kim every other day in my basement sink, so she never really smells like a dog but almost like a pretty woman.

—KENNETH WILLIAMS
CHICAGO, ILLINOIS
🐕 LIL KIM, PIT BULL TERRIER, 1

KAYCEE WAS DIAGNOSED WITH CANCER when she was four years old. Her treatment for the cancer was surgery to remove a tumor followed by three months of chemotherapy. The chemotherapy alone cost me $3,000. She's now nine years old, and between her knee surgeries and autoimmune problems I've spent over $10,000 to keep her alive. Today, she's still a healthy and active dog. I wouldn't think twice about doing the same thing with another dog.

—ROBIN WINDLINGER
FULLERTON, CALIFORNIA
🐕 KAYCEE, BERNESE MOUNTAIN DOG, 9

TIPPY is a retired racing Greyhound adjusting to civilian life.

MILLIE (OWNER)
HARTSDALE, NEW YORK

MY DOG IS MY SON. He is family, not a pet. If somebody comes into my house that my dog doesn't like, he has to go. One guy I started dating and brought home had to leave: My dog started barking and wouldn't stop, so I had to tell this cute guy to leave. Nobody comes before my dog.

—SCHENITA STEWART
GLENWOOD, ILLINOIS
🐕 ALI, AMERICAN STAFFORDSHIRE TERRIER, 3

• • • • • • • •

My dog's name is Brisket. You know how embarrassing it is to call him in public?

—RANA KOLL-MANDEL
GARRETT PARK, MARYLAND
🐕 BRISKET, 60% BEAGLE 40% CHICKEN, 3

SPARKEY WAS A RESCUE. He had already been through four families. He wouldn't even eat his breakfast with the other dogs in the house; I had to put his meals outside until he felt comfortable coming into the house. I decided that I was going to work really hard with him, so I took him to classes to train and socialize him. After a while, the trainer said that there was nothing more she could do. She suggested that since I was training two other shelties in agility at the time, that I should take him back. She said that this dog would never be able to do what the other dogs do. Well, he turned out to be a fantastic little dog and competed in agility, too. He was my prized possession.

—DEBORAH ROHSSLER
GRANADA HILLS, CALIFORNIA
🐕 QUINCY, 13 🐕 MAGGIE MAE, 12
🐕 SPARKEY, 9, SHELTIES
🐕 RAYNE, BORDER COLLIE-AUSTRALIAN SHEPHERD, 5

CIRCUS MAXIMUS

After being with Maximus 24/7 for over a year, I realized I had to return to the normal workplace, which meant we would be separated. As hard as it would be for me, it would be harder for him if he didn't have company. I decided to get a second pug to keep him company. I arranged to see pugs at a local breeder and brought Maximus so I could make sure he approved of my selection. The first pug that came out was the runt of the litter and hadn't been sold because she had some hair loss on the crown of her head. She ran into the room, ignored me, looked at Maximus, who has the personality of a member of the British royal family, and decided he needed a little fun in his life. She went straight for his leash, snatched it from my hand, and proceeded to pull him around the den area. He looked back at me with an expression of "save me from this crazy girl." But I knew that this very little girl would bring joy and happiness into Maximus's life. Since those first days, Indy's carefree behavior has not only enhanced Maximus's life but also changed him from a "proper" Englishman to a well-rounded, outgoing dog.

—Diana Rohini Lavigne
San Francisco, California
🐕 Maximus, 7 🐕 Indy, 6, Black Pugs

RICO is a happy, 11-year-old, black Labrador Retriever with a great attitude.

DENISE FLECK (OWNER)
SHADOW HILLS, CALIFORNIA

SINCE MY DOG IS ALLERGIC to all types of dog food except for the food that is prescribed by his veterinarian, I reward Ali when he gets his shots. I always take him to McDonald's and get him his favorite Chicken McNuggets.

—SCHENITA STEWART
GLENWOOD, ILLINOIS
ALI, AMERICAN STAFFORDSHIRE TERRIER, 3

* * * * * * * *

I BOUGHT A CAR FOR MY DOG. That way, we can jump in the car and go to Connecticut whenever we want to. I have lived in New York City for 14 years and never had a car, so it's a big deal.

—JULIA
NEW YORK, NEW YORK
TRISTAN, MIXED BREED, 1

* * * * * * * *

LADY ALWAYS LOVED THE FOREST, so when she was put to sleep my boyfriend and I took her ashes to Sequoia National Forest. We put her ashes under the General Sherman Tree, which is probably against the law. We actually jumped the fence. We said, "Oh my gosh, we have to get out of here!" My boyfriend wasn't moving so fast; he was sitting there petting the tree, saying, "Bye, Lady." I was yelling, "Come on, we've got to get out of here. We can get arrested for this!" But we were so happy, knowing that she's in her favorite spot.

—LISA MCKEARNEY
LOS ANGELES, CALIFORNIA
LADY, MIXED BREED, 16

WHEN SPARKS WAS A YEAR OLD, he developed something called canine viral papillomas; they looked like little warts around his mouth. I brought him to the vet and the vet assured me that eventually they would fall off and he would build up immunity; sort of like a child and chickenpox. Months went by and they started multiplying. I finally found a dog dermatologist and took him there. He told me that I would need to treat Sparks, at home, with injectable interferon several times a week over a few months. About $3,000 later, the treatment worked; Sparks has been fine ever since. I'm hoping to not have to spend that much money on him again, but if it becomes necessary, I would not hesitate.

—CHIP MASON
LOS ANGELES, CALIFORNIA
🐕 SPARKS, GOLDEN RETRIEVER, 6

Bye, Dog

The time always comes when they leave us. It seems unfair that we will almost always outlive our dog companions, and the time we have together goes by quickly. Often it's up to us to know when the moment has come to say goodbye, and that's never easy, but we do the best we can. And we never forget them.

A COUPLE YEARS AGO MY WIFE AND I got a new dog from a friend of hers. It was this little terrier. It's hard to explain how certain pets get close to you quicker than others do. We had only had the dog about nine months when it got loose and ran out into the road. It was hit by a car and died. I was pretty shook up about it, more than I would have ever imagined. I've had dogs all my life and have seen many of them die. But this one I took hard for some reason. A week later the friend we got the dog from brought over another dog from the same litter. I was so happy I just started crying.

—GEORGE SWAZUK
FLORENCE, KENTUCKY
🐕 TERRIER, 4

• • • • • • • • `

SAM PASSED AWAY AT HOME. I had a veterinarian come to the house and put him down. I always feared doing that with an animal, but it was so much better; it was actually peaceful. I had him on my lap, my kids were there and it wasn't scary at all. I now think it is more humane and it is also so much better for the surviving dog; my other dog, Maggie, got to sniff him, so she knew he was gone. Dogs know when their mates pass on; this way, Maggie got to be there when Sam went to sleep. She knew exactly what happened to Sam.

—JOAN BALLON
LOS ANGELES, CALIFORNIA
🐕 MAGGIE, 14 🐕 SAM, 13, BRITTANY SPANIELS
🐕 SPEX, AUSTRALIAN SHEPHERD, 2

WHEN ALEX TURNED SIX, he was diagnosed with cancer of the spleen and had his spleen removed. After he had his surgery, I would go visit him and he would know when I was about to leave because he would take his paws and wrap them around my arm as if he was trying to get me to stay. Of course, this made me cry. The doctors didn't think he would last long but he recovered for a little while. But when he was seven, he was diagnosed again. The doctors said the cancer had spread and he would have to undergo the same treatment. I was debating what to do: I remembered that the first time he was diagnosed, he looked at me with pleading eyes that seemed to say, "I don't want to go; please help me." This time, over a year later, when he was diagnosed again, he turned away from me and looked at the wall. I knew then that it was too much for him and I had to put him down.

—CAROL CURTISS
LAKE ELSINORE, CALIFORNIA
🐕 SKYE, 5 🐕 FAITH, 3
🐕 ALEX, 7, SHELTIES

• • • • • • • • •

WHEN OUR DOG DIED, it was very bad. She was with us for 18 years. She was family. She couldn't walk. She couldn't see. We wanted her to die on her own, but the vet told us the nicest thing to do was to let her go. We had her cremated and they put her in a pretty box.

—ANGELA COVO
SAN ANTONIO, TEXAS
🐕 GOLDEN RETRIEVER-GERMAN SHEPHERD MIX, 18

CHARLIE WAS 13 when she passed away. To honor her, I go to a spiritual center where they have a blessing of the animals and they also have an animal ministry. Once a year, all of the members get together there. We sit around an altar and there is always a performer there who sings songs for the animals. After the performance, everyone sits around and we show pictures of our animals and tell stories.

—LOUISE BREW
VENICE, CALIFORNIA
🐕 BASIL, 3 🐕 MEMPHIS, 1
🐕 FANNIE, 14 🐕 CHARLIE, 13, SHIH TZUS

• • • • • • • •

MY HUSBAND, HAROLD, died more than 20 years ago, leaving me to live out in the country alone. The first few weeks were especially lonely and sometimes scary, until one day when one of my grandchildren brought me the cutest little ball of fur named Cuddles. This little puppy helped my through some of my darkest days and soon grew to be bigger than me. She was always a faithful companion, going everywhere with me. I'm sure we were a funny sight to see driving down the road: a short, older woman with this big spoiled dog in the front seat. When it was time to let her go, 13 years later, it was very difficult, but she had fulfilled her purpose: to be a best friend to someone who had just lost hers.

—DESSARINE MCNEILL
MAGNOLIA, ARKANSAS
🐕 SASSY, CHOW CHOW-GERMAN SHEPHERD MIX, 8
🐕 CUDDLES, 13

I PUT MY OLD DOG DOWN this past fall and I cried for three days. I decided to put him to sleep because he had a condition where he had trouble swallowing and the vet said he ran the risk of choking to death. That seemed to be a terrible way to die, so I made the date with the clinic. Every day I'd look at my dog and think, "I'm going to kill you in X number of hours." It was terrible. They injected him and all of a sudden he started to choke. Instinctively, I stuck my hand in his mouth to try to take his tongue away and save him and he tried to bite me! Just after snapping at me, he died. I realized he went out like he had lived his life: He was an attack dog until the end.

—J.S.
TORONTO, CANADA
FALCON, PHOENIX, 8, BELGIAN MALINOIS
MIDAS, GERMAN SHEPHERD, 3
ATOM, SHELTIE
FOSTER, AUSTRALIAN CATTLE DOG, 14

• • • • • • • • •

CINDY DIED WHEN SHE WAS SEVEN. We were hysterical. We decided to bury her at the pet cemetery. We chose a casket for her, had a plaque made with her picture on it and the entire family wrote her a letter. On the day of her funeral, we took my son out of school. First we had a viewing where we all got to kiss her and say goodbye. Then we put all of her favorite things, like a pair of my socks, in her casket so that she could have them with her always. We then had a burial service and read her the letter.

—MALCOLM
LOS ANGELES, CALIFORNIA
CINDY, 7 TRACY, 10, BOXERS

WILLIE DEVELOPED A MALIGNANT TUMOR on his hip. We knew we'd probably have to intervene before his body gave out on its own. He was terrified of the vet, so we knew we couldn't put him through the trauma of going there. The emergency animal hospital gave me the name of a woman who had a mobile service. I told her how frightened and nervous Willie was, and how he could be a little aggressive when it came time for a shot. She reassured me that she would be gentle, but I was still anticipating a really rough time. As soon as Willie saw her, though, he started wagging his tail and licking her hand. My husband and I later joked that she wasn't real; if we tried to find her again we'd discover she never really existed, that she was really Willie's angel in disguise. We all sat around holding and petting Willie for a long time. After she gave him the injection, we held him and whispered in his ear how much we loved him, and poof—that was it. His heart stopped and he stopped breathing and there was our big ol' Willie, looking beautiful and free.

—EILEEN GRASING
SAN DIEGO, CALIFORNIA
🐕 WILLIE, 8 🐕 YVAN, 11

DOING THE RIGHT THING

I still remember the moment in the vet's office. Our vet had paused a moment, then said, "I'm willing to do whatever you want me to do. But maybe it's time we start thinking about letting Jake go." Jake, our Aussie, was 8. He had canine epilepsy, and it was wearing him down. The seizures were happening weekly; he was losing control of his bladder. I went home and told my wife. We cried because we knew what we had to do. Jake was our first "child," and it's not natural to kill something you love so much. But when I spoke to my dad, he said, "Pets provide us with unconditional love, and in return they rely on us to make this decision for them." So, I called the vet. I didn't want to bring Jake to his office because the place made him nervous. And my vet wasn't lying when he said he was willing to do whatever I wanted. I told him to meet me at this nearby mountain trail the next day. Jake loved walking there. I stopped at the store on the way and bought Jake's favorite burgers. We arrived at the mountain trail early and had a picnic. When we were finished, I gave Jake a hug and told him I loved him. We put Jake to sleep in the backseat while I held him and talked to him. It was very difficult, but it was the right thing to do, and I don't think I'd choose another way.

—J.W.A.
ATLANTA, GEORGIA
🐕 JAKE, AUSTRALIAN SHEPHERD, 8

AS A CHILD WE HAD A ST. BERNARD-LAB MIX. She was diagnosed with bone cancer in her leg and, due to her size, an amputation was not a suitable remedy. My mother told us that she was going to have to be put to sleep. When the morning came for her to depart, my brother and I handled this quite differently. My brother just pet her head and left for school very quietly. I turned the morning into a party in celebration of her life. I opened every can of food she had left, fed her all the biscuits that were left in the jar, and hoped that she had the absolute best meal of her life.

—HEIDI HENDERSON
KILLINGTON, VERMONT
🐕 EMMA BLU, 1 🐕 LOGAN, 1
🐕 SHASTA DELANEY, 5, BERNESE MOUNTAIN DOGS

* * * * * * * *

WE HAD TO MAKE A DECISION about what to do with Pepper. We decided that the best thing was to put him down. We brought him to our vet, who had just opened up a new hospital. He had a special private room that had a nice couch and was decorated with a lot of special dog and cat toys. It was in a part of the hospital that was away from everything else. We all sat on the floor with him and took pictures. It was like he just went to sleep and we just left him there. It was really sad and at the same time very peaceful. We were just glad that he wasn't suffering anymore.

—CHARLENE VALDEZ
SIMI VALLEY, CALIFORNIA
🐕 OZZIE, KEESHOND, 2
🐕 DR. PEPPER, DALMATIAN, 9

HANNAH HAD A STROKE when she was 13. I took her to the vet and it was pretty clear things weren't going to get better. Even though she was in really bad shape, I couldn't stand the thought of putting her down. But I also didn't want her to keep suffering. I was crying and petting her, talking to her, begging her, saying, "Please don't make me do this. Be a good girl. Put your head down and go to sleep. Please don't make me do this. Please, please go to sleep." Just as the doctor was preparing the injection, she lifted her head up from the table, looked all around the room, put her head down and died. I couldn't believe it! I was completely devastated that she was gone, but it was the most positive thing that could have happened under the circumstances. Hannah did me the biggest favor. She saved me from making a decision I knew I couldn't live with. She was the most loyal, loving dog to the end.

—PETER D. GIBBONS
N. MASSAPEQUA, NEW YORK
🐕 BAILEY, GOLDEN RETRIEVER-RESCUE DOG, 6
🐕 HANNAH, GOLDEN RETRIEVER, 13

RANDY HAD A TOUGH LIFE. He had been abandoned at the age of two and was malnourished when we adopted him. Then when he was about nine years old Randy was diagnosed with diabetes. We had to chase him around with a bowl to catch his urine to test it and determine how much insulin to give him. After a while he started to bite us when he saw us get the bowl. The vet recommended that we put him to sleep, so my son, Cory, dug a grave in the yard. Randy died peacefully at the vet's office, and we brought him back home to bury him in the yard.

—CHAR LAVALETTE
RALEIGH, NORTH CAROLINA
🐕 GRIFFEY, BEAGLE, 8
🐕 RANDY, TERRIER MIX, 9

• • • • • • • • •

MY HUSBAND AND I had two Golden Retrievers, A.J. and Addie, who both passed away when they were 12 years old. My Golden Retrievers used to go swimming at a place called Hidden Pond. When each one of them died we spread their ashes over the pond so they could be in their happiest place. It has been important to us to have some kind of closure with our animals because they are like our children.

—LINDA KORBEL
CULVER CITY, CALIFORNIA
🐕 A.J., 12, 🐕 ADDIE, 12, GOLDEN RETRIEVERS
🐕 COBBER, LABRADOODLE, 16

I'D HAD MY MINI SCHNAUZER for over eight years when I was told he had cancer and only had a week or so to live. I spent the 10 days I had with him taking him to his favorite places, wagon in tow so he could rest. I tried to feed him anything he wanted, but his appetite was all but gone. At his goodbye "party," I let him take a bite of pepperoni pizza, and his eyes lit up again like they used to. When I knew I had to put him down, I decided I definitely was not taking him to the vet, but did not want to have the memory in my home. I then remembered that I had a certificate for a night in the W hotel that was about to expire—and to top it off, he had won the night for us by winning a pet trick contest. He loved going to hotels, too. So, I booked the room and we spent the night together propped up on fluffy pillows. I ordered up his favorite food (a lamb bone) from the fancy hotel restaurant. He could only lick it, but I think he appreciated the effort. The doctor came the next morning and we said our goodbyes as he was put to sleep in my arms.

—BEVERLY ULBRICH
SAN FRANCISCO, CALIFORNIA
🐕 MINIATURE SCHNAUZER

WHEN A PERSON DIES, you have the distraction of a service and funeral and people taking care of you. You don't have that when a pet dies. It's just as important to acknowledge and honor a pet's death as it is a person's, with a call or a card or a visit. When my dog Yvan died, a friend called up and suggested we go to the mountains and have a ceremony. When we got there, we burned some sage. Then we wrote Yvan's name out in sticks put a circle of rocks and flowers around it, and took pictures. On the way home, we stopped at the beach, because Yvan loved the beach and would swim until he practically filled up with water. I also picked up a few rocks because he was obsessive-compulsive about rocks and would rub his nose raw trying to get them out of the ground, even if it took him an hour! I still have one of those rocks; it reminds me of how we celebrated him and remembered how great and hilarious he was.

—EILEEN GRASING
SAN DIEGO, CALIFORNIA
🐕 WILLIE, 8 🐕 YVAN, 11

Best Moment with My Dog

It's often the small stuff you treasure the most—some silly trick, or those ears that perk up with excitement. The wild greeting when you return home from a trip; a quiet minute shared early in the morning. Every dog we've ever owned lives on in our memory of those moments: every dog we live with now helps build our storehouse of moments.

MY HUSBAND AND I drove five hours from our home to pick up Barkly from his breeder. On the drive home Barkly sat on my lap the whole way and dug his little nose into the inside of my elbow. I fell in love with him at that moment, and today, at four years old, he wants to rest his head in the same place every time I'm home.

—KRISTI
LOS ANGELES, CALIFORNIA
🐕 BARKLY, JACK RUSSELL, 4

WHEN I SHOWER IN THE MORNING, I usually leave the bathroom door open a bit. When I get out of the shower and start to dry myself off, Skye comes in and helps me to dry my legs by licking the water off. Whenever she does that I feel like I'm going to have a good day.

—CAROL CURTISS
LAKE ELSINORE, CALIFORNIA
🐕 SKYE, 5 🐕 FAITH, 3
🐕 ALEX, 7, SHELTIES

BOTH MY DOGS ARE VERY LOVING. I can tell them to go kiss Dad and they will go right up and kiss him. They love us and are so attached to us. When the four of us go on walks together, they are like glue. If we stop, they stop. They are not happy unless we are walking together as a group.

—LINDA SMITH
WESTLAKE VILLAGE, CALIFORNIA
🐕 WOODY, BORDER COLLIE, 5
🐕 MILLIE, ENGLISH SHEPHERD, 10

ONE OF MY FAVORITE MOMENTS with my dog was on his 15th birthday, about two months before he passed away. We knew it was going to be his last so we had a birthday party for him and invited a few friends. The entire time our friends were arriving, he stayed seated in our entry-way facing the front door, which he had never done before, and never did afterwards. It was really cute to see him greet all of his guests as they arrived. They were all astonished to see him waiting for them as they entered. He knew it was his big day!

—JAMIE ERNST
DALLAS, TEXAS
🐕 QUINCY, MIXED BREED, 15

• • • • • • • • •

I HAD TO LEAVE MY DOG for two weeks because I volunteered to help in the aftermath of Hurricane Katrina. My twin sister had told me that Ali was staying in the window every night, hoping it would be the night when I came home. I came home one day earlier to surprise everybody. So I went upstairs to my room, and Ali was on the floor, lying on top of my blanket to smell my scent. He glanced at me and put his head back down, thinking I was my sister. About a second later, he realized who I was and started running in circles and barking for 15 minutes. It felt good to know that I was loved, even if it was just a dog.

—SCHENITA STEWART
GLENWOOD, ILLINOIS
🐕 ALI, AMERICAN STAFFORDSHIRE TERRIER, 3

THE FIRST TIME WE WENT TO THE LAKE to go swimming, he did what I call the Snoopy "happy dance" when he got out of the water. He gets excited and runs out of the water in this funny way, like a bunny. It looks like the way dogs run in cartoons—really fast in a circle with his ears flying.

—JULIA
NEW YORK, NEW YORK
🐕 TRISTAN, MIXED BREED, 1

· · · · · · · · ·

MY FIANCÉ AND I GOT WALRUS together, before we were engaged, so we always call her our illegitimate child. When we got engaged, her daddy dressed her up in a little shirt that said, "Will you make me an honest Walrus?" She came out in her shirt and she was dragging a little box behind her with a ring in it. It was a really cute moment.

—AMY HUANG
SANTA MONICA, CALIFORNIA
🐕 WALRUS, YORKIE, 2

· · · · · · · · ·

THERE WAS ONE NIGHT when I had just gone through a breakup and my grandmother sent me Chicken Soup for the Dog Lover's Soul. I started reading it out loud and Chico came up right next to me, right in the crook of my neck, and listened to me read all night. It was the sweetest moment.

—MINDI WALTERS
LOS ANGELES, CALIFORNIA
🐕 CHICO, CHIHUAHUA, 3

My favorite moments are sleeping with Mellow. He's a Pug, and Pugs snore. At first his snoring used to keep me up, but now I can't fall asleep without it.

—MARSHA
LOS ANGELES,
CALIFORNIA
🐕 MELLOW,
PUG, 3

AFTER SPIRIT GOES OUT into the field for a run, we come home and she curls up next to me for a heavy nap. She would run until she dropped if it were up to her.

—TRACY LEE ALLEN
FREDERICK, MARYLAND
🐕 SPIRIT, ENGLISH SPRINGER SPANIEL, 2

• • • • • • • •

HAILEY, a dog in perpetual motion.

HEATHER NELSON (OWNER)
PLYMOUTH, MINNESOTA

• • • • • • • •

AFTER MITZI GETS DONE eating her treats, she jumps on my lap and I rub her back until she burps. Then she just curls up and goes to sleep.

—CONNIE LARRICK
RHOME, TEXAS
🐕 JERRY JOE, 14 🐕 DOC, 12, COCKER SPANIELS
🐕 OSCAR, 12 🐕 RIPPY BEAR, 7, DACHSHUNDS
🐕 MITZI, DACHSHUND-CHIHUAHUA MIX, 7
🐕 BUDDY, TIBETAN TERRIER MIX, 6

STANLEY WOULD LIE NEXT TO ME when I was a little down or sad, and rest his head across my foot. As long as I sat there, he didn't move. If I did have to get up, Stanley would rise up too, and follow me around. Then he'd come back and resume his position.

—PAM DUGGINS
ST. LOUIS, MISSOURI
🐕 STANLEY, COCKER SPANIEL-GOLDEN RETRIEVER MIX

We used to sit on the dock late at night and watch the stars. It was an awesome experience to hang out with him.

—JOHN FOCKE
MARQUETTE, MICHIGAN
🐕 JED, MIXED BREED, 12

LEGS IS JUST A LOVER. She will crawl into anyone's lap and give anyone a kiss. The funny thing is, she does it when you're trying to do something important. Anytime I take a book out she decides that she needs to sit on my lap. I guess she wants to be the center of attention.

—JOANNE BURRIS
TUSTIN, CALIFORNIA
🐕 DANTE, 8 🐕 LEGS, 7
🐕 BABETTE, 10, POODLES
🐕 SPARKY, TERRIER-POODLE MIX, 21

I HAD NEVER BEEN HIKING before I got Tag. I started taking him hiking when he was a puppy, and now I take my other dog Mushu as well. They both love it and it is so fun to conquer a mountain, to get to the end place and be there with my two best friends. We all sit and take it in together. Then we all go home together and collapse.

—GENEVIEVE YATES
CAPE TOWN, SOUTH AFRICA
🐕 TAG, COCKER SPANIEL, 10
🐕 MUSHU, SHIH TZU, 3

• • • • • • • • •

WHEN MY HUSBAND COMES HOME from work every day, he and the dogs have a routine. He walks through the door, sits on the floor, and Hunter and Bodie come running up to him and take turns sitting on his lap. Hunter sits on his lap first because we had him first and he gets jealous. Then Bodie comes and gets next to him and my husband pets him and hugs him.

—SUSIE BROWN
FILLMORE, CALIFORNIA
🐕 HUNTER, 3 🐕 BODIE, 1, SHELTIES

• • • • • • • • •

KODA COMES UP TO YOU and puts her head on your shoulder, like she wants to give you a hug. Then she'll start nibbling on you as if she's trying to clean you.

—TERRI BRINK
SANTA CLARITA, CALIFORNIA
🐕 BUSTER, 4
🐕 KODA, 3, AUSTRALIAN SHEPHERDS

TOBY LOVES TO LIE IN BED with me and he loves to massage me. When I am lying on my stomach, Toby climbs up on my back and presses all of his weight on me, and then he gets up and starts walking on me. Sometimes he walks up and down my body, and sometimes he makes circles. It's the best feeling in the world, and I save a lot of money on bodywork.

—ANONYMOUS
AGOURA HILLS, CALIFORNIA
🐕 TOBY, LABRADOR, 4

* * * * * * * *

COMING HOME FROM WORK, after a long day or from a 15-minute trip to the grocery store, I am always greeted by three dogs beside themselves with glee at seeing me. They shower me with kisses and barks of joy and undying love. It doesn't get much better than that.

—J.
DALLAS, TEXAS
🐕 CHOICEY, 15
🐕 MUFFIN, SHIH TZU-MALTESE MIX, 3

* * * * * * * *

SUNDAYS ARE THE FAMILY'S MOVIE NIGHT and we bring Jada into the living room to watch a movie with us. The kids usually put blankets around her to make her feel comfortable; she's like a second daughter. Sometimes she barks at a funny scene in the movie, and we all just laugh.

—MIA SHANKLIN
CHICAGO, ILLINOIS
🐕 JADA, 1 🐕 LADY, 1

THE BEST TIMES WITH DUFFER were when we would travel together as a family. All five of us would pile into the car for a road trip. He would either lie in the back window (which our sons loved), or he would lie at my feet with his face stuck in the vent, snorting air as it came through. When we stayed in motels and would leave him in the room, he would be sleeping inside the opened suitcase on the bed when we returned. He obviously loved our companionship as much as we loved his.

—CINDY SCHWIE
ROSEVILLE, MINNESOTA
🐕 DUFFER, 15 🐕 ANNIE, 15, MIXED BREEDS

• • • • • • • • •

MY HUSBAND ERIC AND I GOT BAKER as our wedding gift to each other—a black Lab bundle of energy with amazing bloodlines. Two years after we got married, and after we brought Baker home, I got pregnant. Baker knew something was different and would lay his head on my belly. Five days before my due date, we decided to take Baker to the dog park, knowing that soon enough, he would be competing for our love and affection. It was a beautiful sunny Sunday. Baker fetched the ball for more than an hour at the water.

—JULIE
KIRKLAND, WASHINGTON
🐕 BAKER, LABRADOR, 3

Favorite moment: When she sleeps on her back in a spread-eagle position, with her paws up and her tongue out.

—GAVIN BODKIN
BRADFORD, NEW HAMPSHIRE
🐕 SCOTTISH TERRIER

ONE LAZY SATURDAY MORNING my husband and I were snuggling close under the covers. Suddenly, Prissy jumped onto the bed and wedged her cold, wet nose between my husband's face and mine, licking the both of us. She proceeded to squeeze the rest of her body between ours. All we could do was laugh and make room for her in the bed.

—DEBBIE
RINGGOLD, GEORGIA
PRISSY, AMERICAN ESKIMO, 1
GOLD, 12 SIMBA, 1, YELLOW LABS
COCOA, CHOCOLATE LAB, 1

. . . .

KETZI AND I HAVE OUR MORNING ROUTINE. It takes me a while to get out of bed once I wake up. Ketzi knows this, so the first thing she does when my eyes open is jump on me. She rests her two front paws on my shoulder so we are chest to belly; basically, she pins me. Once she's finished with that, she rolls over onto her back so I can scratch her belly. We can't start our day without this routine.

—MARLA
LOS ANGELES, CALIFORNIA
KETZI, POODLE-MALTESE MIX, 6

WHEN OZZIE IS BAD, you can't get mad at him because he just sits there and looks at you with his big brown eyes. He lies on the couch and looks at me like he's thinking, "Is she really going to notice that I'm on the couch when I'm not supposed to be?" Then he waits until I get up and he jumps off and runs outside. He knows he's been bad, but he gives me that look and I just melt.

—CHARLENE VALDEZ
SIMI VALLEY, CALIFORNIA
OZZIE, KEESHOND, 2
DR. PEPPER, DALMATIAN, 9

SPECIAL THANKS

Thanks to our intrepid "headhunters" for going out to find so many respondents from around the country with interesting advice to share:

Jamie Allen, Chief Headhunter

Andrea Fine
Andrea Parker
Andrea Syrtash
Carly Milne
Gloria Averbuch
Helen Bond
Jennifer Doll
Jill Michelle Williams
John Nemo
Kazz Regelman

Ken McCarthy
Linda Lincoln
Lorraine Calvacca
Marie Suszynski
Nancy Larson
Nicole Colangelo-Lessin
Paula Andruss
Shannon Hurd
Stacey Shannon
Staci Siegel

Thanks, too, to our editorial advisor Anne Kostick. And thanks to our assistant, Miri Greidi, for her yeoman's work at keeping us all organized. The real credit for this book, of course, goes to all the people whose experiences and collective wisdom make up this guide. There are too many of you to thank individually, but you know who you are.

Praise for HUNDREDS OF HEADS® *Guides:*

"Hundreds of Heads is an innovative publishing house ... Its entertaining and informative 'How To Survive ...' series takes a different approach to offering advice. Thousands of people around the nation were asked for their firsthand experiences and real-life tips in six of life's arenas. Think 'Chicken Soup' meets 'Zagats,' says a press release, and rightfully so."

—ALLEN O. PIERLEONI
"BETWEEN THE LINES," *THE SACRAMENTO BEE*

"A concept that will be ... a huge seller and a great help to people. I firmly believe that today's readers want sound bytes of information, not tomes. Your series will most definitely be the next 'Chicken Soup.'"

—CYNTHIA BRIAN
TV/RADIO PERSONALITY, BEST SELLING AUTHOR: *CHICKEN SOUP FOR THE GARDENER'S SOUL; BE THE STAR YOU ARE!; THE BUSINESS OF SHOW BUSINESS*

"Move over, 'Dummies'... Can that 'Chicken Soup'! Hundreds of Heads are on the march to your local bookstore!"

—ELIZABETH HOPKINS
KFNX (PHOENIX) RADIO HOST, *THINKING OUTSIDE THE BOX*

"The series ... could be described as 'Chicken Soup for the Soul' meets 'Worst Case Scenario.'"

—RACHEL TOBIN RAMOS
ATLANTA BUSINESS CHRONICLE

Other titles in the HUNDREDS OF HEADS® series:

HOW TO SURVIVE YOUR FRESHMAN YEAR

"This book proves that all of us are smarter than one of us."

—JOHN KATZMAN
FOUNDER AND CEO, PRINCETON REVIEW

"Voted in the Top 40 Young Adults Nonfiction books."

—PENNSYLVANIA SCHOOL LIBRARIANS ASSOCIATION

"This cool new book ... helps new college students get a head start on having a great time and making the most of this new and exciting experience."

—COLLEGE OUTLOOK

HOW TO SURVIVE YOUR FIRST JOB (or Any Job)

Hundreds of gainfully employed, recently out of college, young people offer the best tips, stories, and advice on how to survive your job.

HOW TO SURVIVE A MOVE

"... the wisdom of 600 moving veterans ... "

—THE WASHINGTON POST

"... compiles hundreds of essential moving tips, real-life stories, and quotes ... "

—LIBRARY JOURNAL

HOW TO SURVIVE THE REAL WORLD

"Stories, tips, and advice from hundreds of college grads who found out what it takes to survive in the real world."

—Wendy Zang
Knight Ridder/Tribune News Service

"Perfect gift for the newly minted college graduates on your list."

—Fran Hawk
The Post and Courier (Charleston, SC)

BE THE CHANGE!

"This is a book that could change your life. Read the stories of people who reached out to help somebody else and discovered they were their own ultimate beneficiary. It's almost magic and it could happen to everyone. Go!"

—Jim Lehrer
Executive Editor and Anchor, NewsHour with Jim Lehrer

"An inspiring look at the profound power of the individual to make a positive difference in the lives of others. *Be the Change!* is more than an eloquent tribute to volunteer service—it increases awareness of our shared humanity."

—Roxanne Spillett
President, Boys & Girls Clubs of America

"Civic involvement is an enriching joy, as the people in this book make clear. It's also what makes America so great. This is a wonderful and inspiring book."

—Walter Isaacson
CEO, Aspen Institute

HOW TO LOVE YOUR RETIREMENT

"I found *How to Love Your Retirement* so much fun that I wish I could retire all over again!"

—ROBERT H. POST, M.D.

HOW TO SURVIVE DATING

"Great, varied advice, in capsule form …"

—SALON.COM

"…like having a few hundred friends on speed-dial."

—KNIGHT RIDDER/TRIBUNE NEWS SERVICE

"Reading this book, I laughed out loud. I also decided to decree snippets a most superior art form for dating manuals."

—PAULA BURBA
THE COURIER-JOURNAL

"Whether you're single or not, *How to Survive Dating* will have you rolling with laughter! This isn't your ordinary dating book."

—TRUE ROMANCE

HOW TO SURVIVE YOUR TEENAGER

"…wisdom on each page … provides insight, humor, and empathy…"

—FOREWORD MAGAZINE

VISIT WWW.HUNDREDSOFHEADS.COM

Do you have something interesting to say about marriage, your in-laws, dieting, holding a job, or one of life's other challenges?

Help humanity—share your story!

Get published in our next book!

Find out about the upcoming titles in the HUNDREDS OF HEADS® survival guide series!

Read up-to-the-minute advice on many of life's challenges!

Sign up to become an interviewer for one of the next HUNDREDS OF HEADS® survival guides!

Visit www.hundredsofheads.com today!